E. W. GODWIN   Furniture and Interior Decoration

E·W·GODWIN

Elizabeth Aslin

Furniture and Interior Decoration

JOHN MURRAY

Title-page: E. W. Godwin, *c.* 1880 *(courtesy of Trustees of Victoria & Albert Museum, London)*

First published 1986
by John Murray (Publishers) Ltd
50 Albemarle Street, London W1X 4BD

Design by Malcolm Harvey Young

Printed in Great Britain
by Jolly & Barber Ltd, Rugby, Warwickshire

British Library CIP Data
Aslin, Elizabeth
   E.W. Godwin: furniture and interior decoration.
   1. Godwin, E.W.——Exhibitions
   I.Title
   749.22   NK2542.G6
ISBN 0-7195-4267-7

Contents

Godwin as a Designer of Furniture and Interior Decoration

In the mid-1860s the architect E. W. Godwin (1833–86) moved his growing architectural practice from Bristol to London. Recently widowed, the move also involved Godwin in setting up a new home and by 1867 he had begun to design, for his own use, simple, elegant furniture for much the same reasons as those which had inspired the experiments in furnishing and decoration of William Morris and his friends some ten years earlier. Just as their work had resulted in the establishment of the Morris Firm in 1861, so Godwin's own domestic needs led to a career as a designer of furniture and interior decoration which can be said to have had a significant influence on domestic design in the latter part of the nineteenth century.

Writing of his experiences in retrospect, Godwin described his difficulties in furnishing and decorating his London chambers:[1] 'When I came to the furniture I found that hardly anything could be bought ready made that was suitable to the requirements of the case. I therefore set to work and designed a lot of furniture and with a desire for economy directed that it be made of deal, and to be ebonised. There were to be no mouldings, no ornamental metal work, no carving. Such effect as I wanted I endeavoured to gain, as in economical building, by the mere grouping of solid and void and by more or less broken outline.' In a period when cabinetmaking was synonymous with elaborate carving, gilding and opulent display, Godwin's

intention of basing his designs on the interplay of line and form in an almost oriental manner, was revolutionary. It was equally remarkable for a nineteenth-century architect to admit to considering problems of economy and utility, qualities which recur throughout Godwin's work as a furniture designer both visibly and as a declared intention of the designer. In another article he wrote:[2] 'If we are asked to select the style of furniture from the new designs before us, we require first that the furniture be well lifted from the floor and second that it be as light as is consistent with real strength. But this is not all. It is essential for true domestic comfort in these high-pressure, nervous times, that the common objects of everyday life should be quiet, simple and unobtrusive in their beauty,' an admirable design aim in these similarly nervous times over a century later.

In his own first pieces, as Godwin wrote,[3] 'the scantling or substance of the framing and other parts of the furniture was reduced to as low a denomination as was compatible with the soundness of construction. This was to make possible both cleanliness and movement in the event of a change being required' in the arrangement of the rooms. In fact, the use of cheap deal for his first pieces proved false economy and Godwin was forced to have his own furniture remade in 'mahogany also ebonised and decorated with a few gold lines in the panels'.[4] In the same article the information is provided that amongst the pieces designed in 1867 for his own dining room were the buffet (pl.16 & 17), the coffee table (pl.18) and the chair with the cane seat and back (pl.9) all subsequently 'freely made' by various cabinetmakers and 'Art' furnishers. At the beginning of Godwin's career in the 1860s 'Art' was the monopoly of a small group of aesthetically minded artist-craftsmen, collectors and designers, a position reflected in a letter written to one of his clients in 1873 when he said, 'In common with a few (I am sorry to say a very few) others in my profession, I look upon all my work as Art Work. A building to me is as a picture to a painter or a poem to a poet . . .' However, by the 1880s, such was the success of the ideas of these few pioneers, that every successful retailer or maker of household goods felt it expedient to include the word 'Art' in the description of the furniture, silver or ceramics available for sale. People described themselves as 'going in' for 'High Art', for Art Decoration, Art Embroidery or Art Furniture and Art Manufactures were added to more mundane commercial enterprises. One firm retailed Aesthetic Mixed Seeds for cage birds, and children were involved through the medium of tasteful books and toys. Books and periodicals appeared in profusion and lectures were delivered advising on colour, on design and on every detail of interior decoration. 'Most people are now alive to the importance of beauty as a refining influence. The appetite for artistic instruction is even ravenous.' This is the opening of *The Art of Decoration* by Mrs Haweis, published in 1881 at the height of the Aesthetic Movement. The book was intended as a handbook for aspiring aesthetes and sets the atmosphere of the times. Max Beerbohm, writing some years later of his memories of 1880, suggested that it was to Oscar Wilde 'that Art owed the great social vogue she enjoyed at this time' and that Godwin was 'that superb architect . . . the greatest aesthete of them all'.

Godwin's original pieces of domestic furniture were made by a short-lived and appropriately named Art Furniture Company (see p.22) which, during its brief life in 1867, is recorded as having undertaken repairs to pieces brought from Bristol such as rehinging a Japanese screen. The same furniture designs were later put into production by William Watt (see p.22) and still later by Collinson & Lock (see p.22) and by other firms with or without the designer's permission. These unauthorised copies, a direct result of the growing popularity of 'Art', continued to be made throughout Godwin's career and the coffee table of 1867 was still in production by some firms years after the designer's death. On the credit side, these copies, or as Godwin himself called them, travesties or even caricatures,[5] show the admiration of both customers and the trade for these fresh and original designs. The piracy led William Watt to take the unusual step for an English furniture maker of registering some of Godwin's designs with the Patent Office. Thus the records make it possible to date some designs exactly and some of the finished pieces have the distinction, rare in English nineteenth-century furniture, of being marked with the maker's name. A further source of information on the designs comes from Godwin himself, for in addition to being a prolific professional journalist basing his work on his own experiences, he was something of a hoarder and his surviving personal papers, drawings and notebooks provide an unusually full record of his intentions and methods of work during most of his professional life.

Edward William Godwin was born in Bristol in 1833 and, later, had the conventional architectural training of the day, articled to the city surveyor and coming under the influence of Ruskin whose *The Seven Lamps of Architecture* and *The Stones of Venice* were published in 1849 and 1853 just as Godwin came to maturity. This Gothic influence, though significant, may well have been tempered by that of the great engineer, Isambard Kingdom Brunel (1806–59), who was a friend of his employer and teacher. Godwin's early professional career was similar to that of any other young architect of the time concerned mainly with church restoration, the occasional church school and one or two commercial buildings in Bristol, activities which gave little indication of his eventual influence on the artistic life of the country in his diverse capacities as original architect, designer of theatrical productions, of furniture, wallpaper, textiles and almost every aspect of interior decoration. He soon came to be regarded by his contemporaries as one of the leaders of the Art or Aesthetic Movement together with his friends James McNeill Whistler (1834–1903) and the young Oscar Wilde (1856–1900), for both of whom he designed furniture and interiors.

Apart from creating a heightened interest in interior decoration amongst the aesthetically enlightened, probably the most important long-term effect of the Aesthetic Movement was the introduction into England of a taste for Japanese art. It was this taste which was almost certainly the most important single external influence on the European decorative and applied arts in the second half of the nineteenth century. The influence falls into clearly defined phases so that in the 1850s and 1860s it was a matter for individual collectors and enthusiasts; in the 1870s the fashion was in full swing amongst informed people and in England some aspects of interior decoration and furniture were based on what were believed to be Japanese principles. By the 1880s what had been an art movement had become a fashionable mania and every household from the highest to the most humble contained the required Japanese paper fan or parasol or Wedgwood plate with Japanese-based decoration. Godwin was amongst the small band of enthusiasts of the 1850s and 1860s and probably the first man in England to decorate his house in

the Japanese manner with colour prints on plain coloured walls, with straw matting on the floor on which stood blue and white vases all of which choice items almost certainly came direct from ships coming into Bristol docks from the Far East.

It may be that it was from this source that Godwin obtained various books of Japanese prints notably two slim volumes of Hokusai's *Mangwa* from which he drew his knowledge of Japanese wood construction[6] later used in both furniture design and in interior decoration. Another early collector of Japanese colour prints was Godwin's friend and contemporary the architect William Burges (1827–81) who was a regular visitor to the Godwin home in Bristol. References to Japanese sources appear in many of Godwin's small notebooks and one page of drawings of heraldic badges or crests, taken from an as yet unidentified Japanese book, provided the motifs for almost all his later pattern designs for woven silks and wallpapers (pl.75). Apart from the interest in structure and ornament of Japanese art, probably the most significant influence on all his domestic work was a feeling for spaciousness and for simplicity. It is of some interest that the only piece of furniture predating Godwin's work, incorporating in a very novel way this simple approach to design, was the sofa made by the Morris Firm and shown at the International Exhibition in London in 1862, at which for the first time in Europe the Japanese had a major display. The designer of the sofa, upon which much public scorn was poured, was Dante Gabriel Rossetti, another of the select band of early Japanese collectors (pl.67). The proportions of this design, the variations on the rectangle and the straight lines must derive, as did Godwin's work, from a study of woodwork and domestic fittings as illustrated in Japanese colour prints. Godwin's earlier 'Japanese' furniture is strictly rectilinear and the notebooks include some interesting examples of designs for furniture to be assembled on the unit principle composed of related shelves, cupboards and wardrobes. With increasing experience and confidence, Godwin allowed himself slight variations from the precisely vertical and horizontal. The walnut cabinet (col.pl.8) was made for his own use in about 1876. The sketch design has also survived (col.pl.6) and in this piece there is a subtle outward curve to the supporting members which, though almost imperceptible, gives a much greater feeling of strength than the earlier straight, thin legs. The carved boxwood panels and ivory drawer handles are genuinely Japanese and may well have been acquired from Liberty's East Indian Art Warehouse, opened in Regent Street in 1875. Japanese carved wooden panels were included in their stock and as the business developed special designs and sizes could be ordered from Japan 'to any character of drawing'.[7] From Liberty's earliest days, Godwin had a close association with it and what he called its Anglo-Japanese Warehouse, buying there many of his own household goods and ornaments and eventually, in 1884, becoming consultant and sometime designer to the Liberty Historic Costume department.

However, Japanese art was not Godwin's exclusive study and he is recorded as recommending students of architecture to study everything that they could find but to absorb the information, use it and create their own personal style. This Godwin did certainly, only on rare occasions at the request of clients producing near reproductions based on museum studies such as the Shakespere (sic) Dining-Room Set (pl.68) and the Renaissance-type sideboard (pl.55) both designed for William Watt. In his notebooks there are drawings of furniture from illuminated manuscripts, Gothic and Renaissance architectural detail, Egyptian ornament and from Greek vases and reliefs.

Godwin himself described one of his designs for a chair as based on an 'Old English Example' and it appeared in the Watt catalogue amongst so-called Jacobean designs. With its curved back with rectilinear supports and cane seat it is more closely related to Japanese woodwork than to any English chair (pl.15). The piece serves to prove Godwin's contention that his work was pirated. This particular example was made by Collier & Plucknett of Warwick from a published design. Godwin himself had no recorded dealings with the Warwick cabinetmakers but apart from the illustration in the Watt catalogue of 1877 the chair also appeared in the frontispiece of one of the most popular guides for aspiring aesthetes, *Decoration and Furniture of Town Houses* by R. W. Edis, published in 1881.

Some of Godwin's furniture designs of the early 1880s derive from Greek sources. The 'Greek' chair (pl.64) appears to be based loosely on a series of sketches made from the 'Parthenon marbles' (pl.65) though the precision and detail of these drawings suggest that they were taken from one of the earlier published illustrations rather than from the actual Elgin Marbles. The chair and stool of the sketch-book appear on the east frieze of the Marbles but they are much less clearly defined than Godwin's sketches would suggest. The actual chair is one of a number of later designs for semi-upholstered chairs with extended or elongated backs and subsidiary sloping back support, predating related forms in the work of the Glasgow School in the 1890s and that of Austrian designers around the turn of the century.

The first major building of Godwin's architectural career was Northampton Town Hall for which he won a competition in 1861. Designed with Ruskin's ideas very much in the forefront of his mind, the building has a curiously simple general effect but conversely is very elaborate in detail, the Gothic forms embellished with sculpture and carvings designed and drawn full size, it was reported, by the architect. In 1864 when the work on the building as a whole was well advanced,

Godwin was commissioned to design some furniture which was to be made by Green & King of London (see p.22), a firm describing themselves at that date primarily as artists and decorators. They had been employed on the interior decorations of the building notably the ornately painted roof trusses of the main hall. Of the surviving designs all dated January 1865 (pl. 1 & col. pl. 1) the cupboard, with its painted and carved decoration and ornate metal mounts, is nearest to the French Gothic of the building and seems directly related to a much-illustrated armoire at Bayeux, admired by English designers of the day. The umbrella and hat stands are far more original, possibly due to the fact that no medieval model existed, but the chairs (still in use today) for councillors and Mayor, represent an entirely new approach to design for civic dignatories (pl.2 & 3). The Mayor's armchair is raised literally to a position of dignity by its proportions and not by the conventional elaborate carving nor indeed by the type of carving designed by Godwin three or four years earlier for the same building. The chairs and the accompanying grand council table are all of oak, the main members simple, straight and round in section with painted decoration of stripes and dots very similar to those 'black rings' of the Rossetti sofa. The only concession to the Gothic of the building is the slightly more elaborate decoration of the upper part of the Mayor's chair. The councillors' chairs are three-legged, with semicircular back support and, like the Mayor's chair, are upholstered in dark green leather. Godwin continued to use variations on this form until quite late in his career.

In the late 1850s Godwin had spent some time in Ireland where his elder brother was establishing himself as a civil engineer. While in Ireland Godwin designed some cottages for labourers, a small church at St Johnston in County Donegal, dedicated in 1857, and continued in a small way with the journalism that had been started in the local papers in Bristol, writing on artistic and archaeological subjects for the *Derry Journal*.

These Irish travels and contacts led in 1867 to the largest of Godwin's domestic undertakings when he was commissioned to build Dromore Castle for the Earl of Limerick. This was to be 'Art Work' in the fullest sense since the architect not only designed every aspect of the building internally and externally, but was also involved in the choice of site, selecting with his client the position in which the Gothic castle would have the most impressive and picturesque silhouette. The design of the castle itself was based on the detailed studies of fifteenth- and sixteenth-century fortified remains, explored during Godwin's stay with his brother, but the interior decoration and furniture showed many other influences and in this unlikely setting several of the trade-marks of the Aesthetic Movement made their first appearance. The wall decoration (col. pl. 2) shows the influence of Japan both in colour and in the form and movement of the figure and the peacock, later to become the very symbol of aestheticism, appeared surmounting various pieces of cabinet furniture (pl. 4 & 5). One of the tiny notebooks contains a page of pencil drawings, dated August 1869, of a real sloe in a pot and the head and tail of a real peacock as preliminary studies for the formal wall decoration. This careful use of studies from nature as well as those from historic sources can be found through the whole of Godwin's decorative work. The formalised peacock has a certain rigidity at this stage in its development but it is derived directly from one of the Japanese heraldic badges. From the influences at work in the design for the dining room and its buffet it is easy to understand the commentator who wrote that 'Mr Godwin appears to be perplexed by a divided duty between Ireland and Japan with an occasional leaning to the Mediaeval glories of Europe'.[8]

Despite these confusions in the decorative scheme as a whole, the furniture for the building was most interesting and original, the first important collection designed after his personal domestic work and with no need for economy of material, so that, for example, the chess table did not have a painted playing surface but was inlaid with ebony and ivory (pl.6). The main material used, as a concession to the medieval setting, was wainscott oak and one group of pieces, the sixteen chairs and two armchairs to match (pl.9), were covered with 'common tanned uncoloured leather with a stamped pattern in gold'. This was clearly intended to continue the unsophisticated approach in contrast to the soft silks and velvets and the ebonised mahogany of the drawing room pieces. Sadly only a limited amount of this furniture has survived with its straight supports, simple forms and interesting ornament, but there are drawings and a copy survives of the specification of furniture to be made for the Earl of Limerick, given to William Watt in 1869. This job was to be the basis of a long-standing association between Godwin, the designer, and William Watt, the cabinetmaker, and his successors for Watt himself predeceased Godwin. The Dromore designs included the birch bedroom chair with seat and back support in basket weave cane (pl.7 & 8) originally designed for Godwin's own use and later to be second only to the Morris Sussex chair in popularity in 'enlightened' homes. The Dromore version was in pale or natural birch with painted black lines or rings as were the accompanying whatnots once more echoing the Rossetti sofa of some few years earlier. The design for the councillor's chair at Northampton Town Hall must have provided the basis for the grand, almost medieval, Eagle Chair (pl.5) for Dromore. The basic form remained but the front legs were extended upwards terminating in a virtually life-size eagle's head carved from the solid oak and while the rigidity and angularity of the back support was retained, the two front legs were allowed a slight outward curve, not visible from the front, and

these terminated in carved claw and ball feet. Though originally designed and made for Dromore the 'oak eagle chair in embossed morocco price £10' appeared amongst library furniture in William Watt's published catalogue of 1877 and would seem to have been made in some quantity.

William Watt first appears in records as an upholsterer and cabinetmaker in 1859. After the demise in 1867 of the short-lived Art Furniture Company, Godwin turned to Watt to make and remake some of his own household furniture. Watt also made individual pieces for various clients in the late 1860s as recorded in Godwin's ledgers and in due course achieved the major job of furnishing Dromore. The two men worked closely together, a partnership permanently recorded by the publication of *Art Furniture designed by Edward W. Godwin FSA and manufactured by William Watt, 21 Grafton Street, Gower Street, London, with hints and suggestions on domestic furniture and decorations.* This long-winded title comes from the Japanese-style cover of their catalogue published in 1877 and dedicated to HRH Princess Louise, for whom Godwin designed, decorated and furnished a studio soon after. The frontispiece of the catalogue has a title mentioning 'and others' as responsible for some of the designs but there is no further reference to other designers and Godwin's personal diaries record that he finished his drawings for the catalogue on Christmas Day 1876. The explanatory text is by Godwin and by Watt himself who by this time was describing his premises as 'Art Furniture Warehouse' and had opened cabinet works in additional premises in Camden Town, one of the traditional cabinetmaking areas of London. The catalogue has twenty plates illustrating every aspect of domestic design in which Godwin was involved. William Watt's comments on the individual pieces draw attention to their long association and the origins of the designs so that in reference to the buffet shown on Plate 6 (pl.12) it is explained that it 'was originally made for Mr Godwin in black and gold with a curtain of gold embroidery on yellow satin' and there are a number of examples of 'economic furniture' intended for gentlemen whose means are limited. In addition these gentlemen were offered toilet sets designed by Godwin and made for Watt by the reputable pottery firm of William Brownfield of Cobridge in Staffordshire. Sketches for the pottery appear in the notebooks in various forms and colours (pl. 48) and Watt may have been the agent through whom wallpaper designs were commissioned to be manufactured by Jeffrey & Co, the most distinguished printers of the time who had been responsible for the first of William Morris's papers. The Watt catalogue shows seven papers and three borders in various combinations including the peacock and the flowering bamboo (pl. 77 & col. pl. 16) though it would appear that there were many other Godwin-designed wallpapers on the market. Five years before the production of the Watt catalogue, in 1872, a house was designed and decorated, but not in this instance furnished, by Godwin for Earl Cowper in the Sherwood Forest. The specifications for the various tradesmen involved in the work instructed the paperhanger that all the bedrooms, dressing rooms, usual offices and the hall and stairs were to be papered with 'papers to be had of Messrs Jeffreys and to be Mr Godwin's patterns'. These wallpapers have long disappeared which makes it impossible to identify all the Godwin designs from amongst the great Jeffrey production of the period. The surviving records indicate that Godwin was in contact with Jeffrey & Co from 1871 until January 1880; that papers, other than those in the 1877 catalogue, were designed for William Watt and registered by him with the Patent Office (pl. 83 & 84); and that Godwin worked for two other wallpaper manufacturers in the 1870s: Lightbown Aspinall & Co and a long-vanished firm called Toleman. This leaves a considerable volume

of pattern design which has yet to be positively identified.

In addition to wallpaper and jugs and basins, Watt offered in his catalogue other goods made presumably by contractors to his orders. These included stained glass windows, 'stained glass blinds for plate glass windows' and some metal furniture. His own new premises apparently made it possible for him to accept contracts for choir stalls and other church furnishings and estimates for 'staircases and interiors' were offered on the basis of the Japanese hall on Plate 1 of the catalogue.

Possibly the most influential of Godwin's furniture designs were those that were made for William Watt for a group displayed at the Universal Exhibition in Paris in 1878, in which Whistler collaborated. Godwin and Whistler had first met in 1863, inspired by their mutual enthusiasm for Japanese art, and were in close touch for the rest of Godwin's life, and the association continued in the sense that Whistler married Godwin's widow, Beatrice. Godwin's sketch-books include several drawings of Whistler and his associates and the Whistler collection in the University of Glasgow includes sketches and notes by Godwin; in one instance these little drawings appear with careful notes on a copy of the prospectus produced by Whistler to publicise his famous Peacock Room (pl. 30), now in the Freer Gallery, Washington. The immediacy of the influence of his friend's latest decorative scheme which the hand-out claimed was based on 'The Eye of the Peacock' can be seen in two Godwin designs based on birds' eyes produced after his visit to the rich gold and blue room (col. pl. 15).

It is difficult to establish the extent of Godwin's and Whistler's co-operation in some of the projects for interior decoration and for the exhibitions with which they were both associated, particularly since much of the surviving written evidence is somewhat partisan. However the division of responsibility on the Paris exhibition stand seems fairly clear. Godwin designed the furniture for the exhibitor, William Watt. In the course of correspondence with Watt, Godwin suggested that Whistler should undertake the painting of the dado on the stand, probably inspired by his admiration for the panelled dado of the Peacock Room completed earlier in the same year, 1877. Godwin's suggestion was accepted and the project developed until it was a combined effort by the architect and the painter, with abstract painting complementing the furniture design. On this occasion Godwin abandoned his favourite ebonised wood and worked in light coloured mahogany. The whole exhibit was in related colours officially described as a harmony in yellow, but by one critic, at least, as 'an agony in yellow'.[9] On the evidence of the one known surviving piece, the centre cabinet (col. pl. 9), this was a most unfair description. Textures and tones varied but yellow in one tone or another was used for everything: the carpet yellow ochre, the upholstery, pale citron yellow and the furniture bright mahogany with the larger pieces and the wall panels painted in yellows and principally in gold based on the Japanese cloud or scale form which can be seen clearly in a contemporary photograph (pl. 28). While Whistler may well have been responsible for the idea of a symphony in yellow, it is clear that Godwin made all the furniture designs. Some of the individual pieces had been in production earlier, such as the upholstered lounging chair (pl. 33 & 34) the design for which had been registered with the Patent Office in London by William Watt in 1876, two years before the exhibition. The sketch design for the central feature (pl. 29) and another design for a chair are dated September 1877. This predates by some three or four months the approach to Whistler on the subject of the painted dado. Commented upon in the artistic and architectural press, the 'Anglo-Japanese' furniture was illustrated in the *Building News* of 14 June 1878, with a text explaining in some detail the slight variations available to purchasers such as an increased number of spindles in the chair arms and brass feet or shoes for the table legs. The smaller pieces of furniture presumably were sold in Paris but the central feature returned to England. The lower part was immediately converted from a fireplace to a cupboard with doors painted by Whistler. Designed purely for eye-catching exhibition purposes, it was much larger than any other known piece by Godwin and understandably remained in Watt's showroom certainly until four years after the exhibition as was reported by a contemporary writer in his glowing account of the association of Godwin and Watt:

'True lovers of art, as distinguished from the mass of those who have lately been compelled by fashion to bow at her altars, will be well repaid for a visit to the establishment of Mr William Watt of Grafton Street, Gower Street. The furniture there shown is hardly, from the nature of it, for the million. It is not machine made and cheap, produced to meet a demand by the ton; nor is it, like too much of the work of this real revival, a mere careful reproduction of old designs of Chippendale, Adam or Sheraton. It is all of modern design and adapted to modern uses. Two rooms are shown in which the furniture is entirely from the designs of Mr E. W. Godwin, FSA. These are original and very tasteful and the workmanship in all cases excellent. A large cabinet decorated by Mr Whistler's hand may be seen here. Mr Watt together with Mr Godwin has a good claim to be considered the originator of the great revival in the domestic arts which, with all allowances for its vagaries, is an established fact. He has never departed from the standard set before himself at the first and his shop has unique and peculiar interest whilst we begin to complain in other places of the sameness in the designs to be met and of the poverty and scamping in workmanship.'[10]

Just as Godwin and Whistler must both have been stimulated by each other's work and ideas so a similar creative relationship may have existed between Godwin and the American architect, H. H. Richardson (1838–86). Five years younger than Godwin, Richardson was very much interested in English design and in particular it is recorded was an admirer of the early architectural work of Burges and of Godwin. He made a number of trips to England but there is no evidence of personal contacts. However, some of the Richardson furniture, notably pieces for a library at Woburn, Massachusetts (pl. 35), are so like Godwin's designs both in form and in detail that the similarity must be more than coincidence. One explanation is that the Woburn furniture was made in 1878, a year after the publication of the Watt catalogue and at the same time as the Paris exhibition. On the other hand, a sketch design for a house in one of Godwin's notebooks is dated January 1877 and inscribed 'Richardsonian'. This seems the first tentative clue to the meeting of the two architects or at least an indication of mutual admiration.

In July 1872 Godwin entered into what was intended to be an exclusive agreement to design furniture of all kinds and to make decorative schemes for the firm of Collinson & Lock, Art Furnishers (see p. 22). Collinson and Lock had both trained at the reputable establishment of the conventional cabinetmakers, Jackson & Graham. In 1870, no doubt sensitive to the rising tide of aesthetic taste in interior decoration, they set up their own business and in 1871 published their first catalogue of furniture mostly to the designs of the architect T. E. Collcutt, to coincide with the International Exhibition held in London that year in which the emphasis was on furniture and the cabinetmaking trade. Collcutt's best-known and most successful design at this exhibition was an ebonised cabinet with painted decoration by the established watercolourist and colleague of Whistler,

Albert Moore. This piece, considered by the trade press to be something of a novelty, caught the mood of the times and led to a veritable flood of ebonised work with more or less artistic painted decoration. In addition to the London piece Collinson & Lock showed two cabinets exactly similar in form at the International Exhibition in Vienna in 1873 and the Philadelphia Centennial Show in 1876. The former had painted decoration by Edward Burne-Jones and the latter, acquired by the Metropolitan Museum in New York, had decoration based on the Burne-Jones designs but painted by his pupil, Charles Fairfax Murray. It was Murray who was responsible for the painting of the 'Lucretia' corner cabinet designed by Godwin for Collinson & Lock in 1873 and shown at various subsequent international exhibitions (col. pl. 18 & pl. 42). The second half of the nineteenth century was punctuated by these international events described by one contemporary writer as 'those great Olympic Games which in our modern language we call universal exhibitions'.[11] The stated occasion for these events varied but all were highly competitive, with medals and a good press meaning more orders for the exhibitors. After only about a year with Collinson & Lock, Godwin was one of their star performers in Vienna with his exhibits ranging from the light and simple artistic to a sideboard the decoration of which included tortoiseshell, brass, 'bright red wood' and ebony, and there was also a rather elaborate reading desk cum portfolio stand (pl. 25). However diverse the display it did lead to orders for furniture most notably chairs and other work for Prince Esterhazy (pl. 26 & 27), the designs for which Godwin seems to have taken by hand to Vienna recording in his diary the meeting with Lock there in the Golden Lamb Hotel, Leopoldstrasse.

The agreement with Collinson & Lock involved a retainer of £450 per annum paid in monthly instalments quite regularly as far as can be seen

the architect designed the furniture, chose the wall-papers, often of his own design, supervised the mixing of the paint and finally selected pictures and ornaments. Many of Godwin's little sketches show that the interiors were in his mind at the earliest stages of a design (pl. 70 & 71). Sections through designs for villas of modest proportions show details of suggested wall decoration for 'Japanese' fireplaces or overmantels. Apart from the complete Art Work of a Godwin-designed house, numbers of schemes were undertaken in existing buildings ranging from his own houses to rather grander work such as that for a house in Lowndes Square for Gladys, Countess of Lonsdale; an even more splendid design for Mrs Langtry naturally using the lily as the main motif; and probably the most interesting and certainly the most 'aesthetic' scheme for Oscar Wilde's house in Tite Street, Chelsea.

Unfortunately none of the domestic interiors from Godwin designs exists today with the exception of one or two modest houses where the structural and decorative form survives though not the original decoration. This was to some extent inevitable since two of the prime elements in any Godwin decor were perishable wallpaper and plain though subtle paintwork. Some interiors, such as that of Whistler's White House in Tite Street, Chelsea, vanished almost as soon as they were completed. This house, one of Godwin's most complete works, was designed in 1878. Whistler's unfortunate financial situation meant that he lived in the house for less than a year and the new owner who purchased the White House in 1879 immediately made radical internal alterations. Other houses in various parts of the country survived well into this century, the decorative schemes eventually being replaced or the houses demolished. However, on the credit side, Godwin's ideas of simple and elegant interior decoration made such a mark in their own day that a number of people recorded their impressions

and Godwin himself wrote of his views on interior decoration and colour as fully as he did on many other subjects. In addition a few estimates for jobs survive together with instructions to painters and other craftsmen and these, with the notebooks, make it possible to visualise at least some of the aesthetic interiors.

In 1874 Godwin decorated a conventional London terrace house for his own occupation and in a series of articles in the *Architect* two years later he gave detailed descriptions of every room, even to his exact recipe for the mixing of the paint. For example in the drawing room he used 'a rather dark-toned yellow of which yellow ochre is the base, but combined with white, sprinkled with gamboge, Prussian blue and vermilion'. This was the colour used for the main woodwork of the room below the dado. The walls above this level were divided vertically by pilasters and a framework for a frieze 'painted in a pale grey green (that green sometimes seen at the stem end of a pineapple leaf when the other end has faded – indeed I may as well confess that most of the colours in the rooms have been gathered from the pineapple).' This interest in the subtleties of colour of the faded pineapple are recorded in another of the detailed studies in the notebooks. The entrance hall and all the ground-floor rooms of the house were un-carpeted and the bare floors oiled and waxed. The dado was of Indian matting and the upper part of the wall covered with a paper in a conventional pattern in umber and vellum colour. The ceiling was also pale, creamy vellum colour and all the paintwork a light red. It is clear that the aim of all this careful thought was to produce an air of calm and simplicity and Godwin prefaces the description of each of his rooms with notes on the mistakes made in the average house from violent over-florid carpets to 'a very objectionable habit with some people . . . is to fill up their drawing rooms with furniture and knickknacks until a short-sighted person is placed in constant peril.' Godwin's correction of these common errors and the overall effect was so unusual that it was recorded by various contemporaries, such as the actor Sir Johnston Forbes-Robertson who remembered that 'the floor was covered with straw-coloured matting and there was a dado of the same material. Above the dado were white walls and the hangings were of cretonne with a fine Japanese pattern in delicate grey blue. The chairs were of wicker with cushions like the hangings and in the centre of the room was a full sized cast of the Venus de Milo before which was a small pedestal holding a censer from which was curving round the Venus, ribbons of blue smoke.'[12] According to the designer there were also a few Japanese fans against the skirting and also on the ceiling, some Japanese vases and a few lightweight pieces of furniture. 'No description, however, except perhaps that which may be conveyed in the form of music, can give an idea of the tenderness and, if I may say so, the ultra-refinement of the delicate tones of colour which form the background to the few but unquestionable gems in this exquisitely sensitive room. I say *sensitive* for a room has a character that may influence for good or bad the many who may enter it, especially the very young.'[13] These few words contain the essence of the aesthetic approach to design or Art Work as Godwin called it, with the implied interrelationship of the arts and everyday life. None but an aesthete would have contemplated the description of his London drawing room in terms of music. These rooms and another decorated in shades of blue were designed while Godwin was living with the actress, Ellen Terry, and in her memoirs she records the exceptional artistic upbringing of their two children clearly explained by Godwin's concern for the influence on the very young of their surroundings. 'They were allowed no rubbishy picture books but from the first Japanese prints and fans lined the nursery walls'[14] and the children wore tiny kimonos, looking as Japanese as all that surrounded them.

When Oscar Wilde married in 1884 he took the lease of a modest conventional house at 16 (now 33) Tite Street, Chelsea, where Godwin had already built and furnished several houses and studios for clients and friends. A full description of the interior of this house survives[15] and records, amongst other details, Godwin's particular enthusiasm for the design of individual rooms based on the variation on a single colour. The best-known example was the harmony in yellow at the 1878 Paris Exhibition but even earlier in 1874 he records a yellow or gold scheme for himself: 'In and round the buffet a certain golden atmosphere was attained by the use of different yellows. Besides the gold lines on the panels there were a large round brass tray in the shadow, a large imperial yellow jar, two smaller yellow jars from Cannes, a bit of Chinese gold embroidery on yellow satin and some yellow-green plates.'[16] The most subtle room in Oscar Wilde's house had shades not of yellow but of white and this at a time when the general practice was to mix a variety of positive designs and sombre colours in one room irrespective of lighting or outlook. Oscar Wilde described the chairs for the dining room as 'sonnets in ivory' and the table as a 'masterpiece in pearl' and Godwin's instructions for the decorators – not, on this occasion, required to read Chaucer or Shakespeare first – were 'the whole of the woodwork to be painted enamel white and the walls pt in oils enamel white and grey to the height of 5 ft 6 ins. The rest of the walls and ceiling to be finished in lime white with a slight addition of black to give the white a greyish tone.' The colours of each room are carefully itemised and required to be of the highest quality with the work supervised by the architect. From the records of one of the other studio houses in Tite Street, that for Frank Miles, also an artist and a Japanese enthusiast, it would seem that each part of each scheme was approached with a perfectionist's care. Having provisionally decided on a paint colour 'a charming red compounded of light red, black and white and yellow' against which it seems blue and white china were expected to look well, the paint was applied in a small area only so that the architect could study the effect of natural light in the room before finally committing himself. The Miles studio house was not merely built and decorated to the architect's requirements, but in this case the Art Work went to the lengths of fully equipping every room from the studio to kitchen, fitments including a dozen claret glasses to be bought from Powells of Whitefriars.

In 1878 in the midst of his studio work in Tite Street, Godwin was commissioned by another artist, in a very different setting, to design and equip a sculpture studio. The job came from HRH Princess Louise, the sculptress daughter of Queen Victoria who lived at Kensington Palace and wanted a studio in her garden. There had been some contact between the architect and his patron since the Watt catalogue of 1877 was dedicated to the Princess, but Godwin obtained this job, important for his reputation if modest in scale, in the face of some competition. The building itself was illustrated in the *British Architect*, in December 1880, long after it was finished but the interior designs were never published. It was a simple shape with the large studio windows but with domestic touches in the fireplaces and the ante room (pl.73). In the setting of a Royal Palace Godwin seems to have been encouraged by his own taste and that of the Princess to unusual simplicity of decoration. In one part of the correspondence it was suggested that the lower wall decoration might be of a severe and simple design founded on the square and the final drawing for the studio fireplace has a note on it indicating the use of painted deal, the cheapest of woods and that there should be as ornament 'rough plaster with scratchings as if in preparation for another coat'. This area of rough plaster, in a supposedly Japanese manner, was to provide the setting for Princess Louise's Oriental ceramics.

It has to be remembered that the design of furniture was only a part of Godwin's many and diverse activities as architect, journalist, antiquary, Shakespearean scholar and, as one contemporary writer said, 'as a setter of plays unsurpassed'. However, his contemporaries did see him as an innovator in the field of furniture design, admitting that in their view individual designs erred 'sometimes, we think, in what we might term over-elegance, the proportions often too slight for strength. His Anglo-Japanese designs were more suited to a proper use of wood design than any modern furniture.'[17] The same writer expressed in more practical terms Godwin's views on Art Work: 'He for ever pleaded for a greater reconciliation between the decorative and the constructive arts, and contended that the decorator and the cabinet-maker should be as much subject to the architect as any other contractor about the building.' This view was the foundation of much of the work of the Arts and Crafts architects and designers who laid emphasis on the production of a complete domestic setting for their clients. Shortly after Godwin's early death an anonymous contemporary wrote that 'his influence was greater than that of many men whose names are better known to the public. Long before any attempt was made to popularise art, he recognised that houses need not be ugly in order to be comfortable. We are still, alas! in an age of stucco and bastard art but the little that has been done to beautify our domestic surroundings is mainly due to him.'

In his furniture work Godwin's importance was that he was the first nineteenth-century designer to be concerned primarily with function and not with superficial style and it was for this reason that his work was admired particularly by the Austrian and German designers at the end of the last century. Some twenty years after Godwin's death the German art historian, Hermann Muthesius, wrote of the lightness and elegance of his furniture and saw it as containing the seeds of the innovative new designs made in Europe in the last decade of the nineteenth century and the first of the twentieth.[18]

Notes

1 *Architect*, 1 July 1876, p.5.
2 *Globe*, 15 June 1872.
3 *Architect*, 1 July 1876, p.5.
4 *Architect*, 1 July 1876, p.5.
5 *Art Furniture designed by Edward W. Godwin FSA and manufactured by William Watt, 21 Grafton Street, Gower Street*. London, 1877. Preface
6 *Building News*, 12 February 1875, p.173.
7 *Eastern Art Manufactures and Decorative Objects*. Liberty & Co, 1881.
8 *Building News*, 11 October 1872, p.291.
9 *Magazine of Art I*, 1878, p.116.
10 *Artist*, vol III, 1882, p.387.

11 *Chef d'Oeuvre of the Industrial Arts*, Philipe Burty. London, 1869, p.172.
12 *A Player under Thee Reigns*, J. Forbes-Robertson. London, 1925, p.66.
13 *Architect*, 5 August 1876, p.73.
14 *The Story of My Life*, Ellen Terry. Boydell Press, 1982, p.50.
15 'Oscar Wilde and His Architect', *Architectural Review*, March 1951, p.175.
16 *Architect*, 1 July 1876, p.5.
17 *British Architect*, 15 October 1886, p.347.
18 *The English House*, Hermann Muthesius. London, 1979, p.157. (*Das Englische Haus*, Berlin, 1904.)

Cabinetmakers with whom Godwin worked

ART FURNITURE COMPANY, 25 Garrick Street, Covent Garden, London.

Advertised November 1867 'are prepared to supply at ordinary trade prices, domestic furniture of an artistic and picturesque character, designs by C. Eastlake, A. W. Blomfield and W. Godwin and other architects'.

COLLINSON & LOCK, 109 Fleet Street, London.

Godwin was in theory working as a designer exclusively for C. & L. from July 1872 for about three years. During this period he was paid a monthly retainer and the designs included furniture, complete interior decorative scheme, textiles and wallpapers. Many of the furniture designs continued in production for some years after the termination of the contract.

COX & SON, 3 Southampton Street, Strand, London.

Gothic, domestic and artistic furniture manufacturers, upholsterers, painters and decorators. Furniture designs ordered 1876.

GILLOW'S, Lancaster & Oxford Street, London.

Furniture, decoration and architectural work 1874 to 1876.

C. GREAVES, 40 Queen's Road, Chelsea, London.

Cabinetmaker employed by Godwin 1882.

GREEN & KING, 23 Baker Street & 100 New Bond Street, London.

Decorative artists, upholsterers, cabinetmakers and general contractors. Originally employed on painted decoration and furniture for Northampton Town Hall, 1861.

W. A. & S. SMEE, 89 Finsbury Pavement, London.

Wholesale Cabinetmakers. Designs supplied by Godwin and the furniture shown at Furniture Trades Exhibition, London 1883.

WILLIAM WATT, 21 Grafton Street, Gower Street, London.

Art Furniture Warehouse. First worked with Godwin 1867/8 and continued until 1885/6. Published in 1877 the catalogue *Art Furniture designed by E. W. Godwin FSA and manufactured by William Watt, 21 Grafton Street, Gower Street, London, with hints and suggestions on domestic furniture and decorations.*

WAUGH & SONS, 65 Tottenham Court Road, London.

Carpet manufacturers, upholsterers, gilt and decorative furniture, easy chairs, couches and centre ottomans. Quantity of furniture designs ordered from Godwin for stock 1876 together with one complete interior scheme and other work including carpets 1881.

Catalogue

All the drawings, designs and objects illustrated are the work of E. W. Godwin except where otherwise stated. The drawings, sketchbooks, notebooks and other documentary material in the collections of the British Architectural Library and the Victoria and Albert Museum were all given to those institutions by Edward Godwin, the son of the architect. The sketchbooks mentioned in the catalogue are mostly Henry Penny's Patent Notebooks and the average page size is 16cm × 10cm.

COLOUR PLATES

1 Northampton Town Hall Furniture. Bookcase and umbrella stand signed E. W. Godwin Arch.t. The written instructions for the maker indicate the use of iron door furniture, painted decoration and birchwood for parts of the umbrella stand. The pieces were made by Green & King in about 1863 who were also responsible for the extensive painted wall decorations in Godwin's first major building dated 1860–5.
Pencil, ink and watercolour
Collection: *Victoria and Albert Museum*
E.622–1963

2 Design from a sketchbook for wall decoration for Dromore Castle, County Limerick, Eire. Dating from 1869 this is the earliest example of Japanese influence in Godwin's interior decorative schemes.

The castle, based on a close study of fifteenth- and sixteenth-century remains in Ireland, was built for the 3rd Earl of Limerick between 1866 and 1873. Gothic in form it was decorated internally with Oriental porcelain set on Godwin furniture and should have been complemented by wall decoration painted by Henry Stacy Marks, RA, much of which was 'not entirely carried through' as the result of problems with damp.
Pencil and watercolour. 1869
Collection: *Victoria and Albert Museum*
E.491–1963

3 Design from a sketchbook devoted to Japanese-inspired subjects. Inscribed with colour notes and instructions but the place of the interior scheme is unknown.
Pencil and watercolour, about 1875
Collection: *Victoria and Albert Museum*
E.280–1963

4 Design from a sketchbook for a small display cabinet for Oriental ceramics. Inscribed 'Geflowski' and 'Home at 4 Club at 7' – typical of the diary form of many of the small notebooks.
Pencil and watercolour, about 1876
Collection: *Victoria and Albert Museum*
E.233–1963

5 Design for a fireplace and overmantel from a sketchbook, inscribed 'Persian Romance' and

probably intended for the house of Frank Miles in Tite Street, Chelsea.
Pencil and watercolour, about 1878
Collection: *Victoria and Albert Museum*
E.233–1963

6 Design from a sketchbook for the 'Monkey Cabinet' with a version of the coffee table first designed in 1867. Inscribed $\frac{1}{2}$ in. scale and £18. The cabinet was designed by Godwin for his own use. (See also col.pl.8.)
Pencil and watercolour, about 1876
Collection: *Victoria and Albert Museum*
E.233–1963

7 Design from a sketchbook for a display cabinet in a room setting inscribed 'A.J.Cab (A) Watt Exhibition Cabinet'. One of many Anglo-Japanese designs made for William Watt, in this case probably for the Universal Exhibition, Paris, 1878.
Pencil and watercolour, about 1878
Collection: *Victoria and Albert Museum*
E.233–1963

8 'Monkey Cabinet': walnut with Japanese carved boxwood plaques inset and Japanese carved ivory handles in the form of monkeys. Made for the designer's own use probably by William Watt, 1876.
Provenance: Edward Godwin, the designer's son by whom bequeathed
Collection: *Victoria and Albert Museum*
Circ.34–1958
H. 192 cm; W. 198 cm; D. 50 cm

9 'Butterfly Cabinet': bright mahogany with painted decoration of Japanese cloud motifs and butterflies in shades of yellow and gold. Designed by E. W. Godwin in 1877 as the central feature of the William Watt stand at the Universal Exhibition, Paris, 1878. The decoration painted by J. A. McNeill Whistler, 1878. The lower doors are contemporary replacements of the firegrate and tile surround of the original design. Illustrated in the *Building News*, 14 June 1878.
Collection: *Hunterian Art Gallery, University of Glasgow*
H. 298 cm; W. 277.2 cm

10 Cabinet: satinwood with brass mounts, ivory handles and a carcass of mahogany; the upper doors decorated with four gilt and painted panels of figures representing the seasons. The paintings, executed probably by Godwin's wife Beatrice, are based on four of twelve sketches of figures representing the months reproduced to illustrate the *British Architect Kalender* in 1881. The brass-framed lattice openings on the lower doors were taken from the *Hokusai Mangwa*, vol 5, 1816, a copy of which was owned by Godwin and was also used as a source of illustrations for an article on 'Japanese Wood Construction' in the *Building News* 1875. Made by William Watt probably about 1877.
Collection: *Victoria and Albert Museum*
W.15–1972
H. 177.8 cm; W. 128.3 cm; D. 40.6 cm

11 Design from a sketchbook for a cabinet and stand in a room setting. Inscribed 'Beatrice Cabinet Stand Watt Sep paid' and dimensions. Made by William Watt, 1879. The figure panels of the Four Seasons painted by Godwin's wife Beatrice, described in the *Building News*, 31 October 1879, as 'a daughter of the late Mr Birnie Philip, the sculptor'. The illustration and text indicate that the cabinet was of red mahogany with yellow mahogany trim, hinges and handles of thin brass and the painted panels set in a surround of mirror glass.
Collection: *Victoria and Albert Museum*
E.233–1963

12 Designs from a sketchbook for decorative panels for a cabinet with varied antiquarian influences.
Pencil and watercolour, about 1878
Collection: *Victoria and Albert Museum*
E.286–1963

13 Design for a panel of stained or painted glass. Illustrated Plate 18 of *Art Furniture*, William Watt's catalogue of 1877 in which the cabinetmaker undertakes to provide estimates for glass.
Pencil and watercolour, about 1877
Collection: *Victoria and Albert Museum*
E.517–1963

14 Design for one of three roundels of stained glass based on hart's tongue fern, lilies and corn inscribed with partially obliterated notes on size and price.
Pencil and watercolour on Whatman paper watermarked 1867
Collection: *Victoria and Albert Museum*
E.519–1963

15 Designs from a sketchbook containing designs for textiles and wallpapers. Based on birds' eyes and inscribed 'Eagles Eye' and 'Cassowary' these designs seem likely to have been inspired by Godwin's first visit to Whistler's Peacock Room in February 1877. The printed handout describing the scheme said that the main pattern source for the decoration was 'the Eye of the Peacock'.
Pencil and watercolour, 1877
Collection: *Victoria and Albert Museum*
E.241–1963

16 Design for wallpaper showing bamboo leaves and formalised Japanese flowers. Inscribed 'Wall Decoration November 1872', the paper was printed by Jeffrey & Co, 1872, and the payment for the design recorded in Godwin's ledger. Illustration of this design in William Watt's *Art Furniture* (Plate 20) and other sources show it used both as a frieze and a filling.
Watercolour on tracing paper, 1872
Collection: *Victoria and Albert Museum*
E.515–1963
52.5 cm × 52.5 cm

17 Figure in a room setting from an undated notebook showing an Anglo-Japanese decorative scheme, as described in some of Godwin's own writing on interior decoration. The figure in a soft flowing dress, sits on an ebonised chair on best plain Indian matting, an Oriental rug laid on it, the decoration in panels Japanese-inspired and the two ceramic objects, an Oriental blue and white vase and a William de Morgan dish, dating from the mid 1870s.
Pencil and watercolour, about 1876
Collection: *Victoria and Albert Museum*
E.286–1963

18 'Lucretia' corner cabinet: rosewood with incised and painted decoration and metal fittings designed, 1873. Made by Collinson & Lock, the decoration painted by Charles Fairfax Murray showing on the centre panel 'Lucretia' and on the small side panels, figures of 'Castitus' and 'Fortitudo'. The study for the 'Lucretia' panel originally owned by John Ruskin, exhibited at the Universal Exhibition, Paris, 1878. Stamped Collinson & Lock and Edwards & Roberts, the former as maker, the latter as subsequent dealer.
Collection: *Michael Whiteway*
H. 188 cm; W. 58.5 cm; D. 78 cm

MONOCHROME PLATES

1 'Furniture at Town Hall Northampton': designs for trestle table, Mayor's chair and councillors' chairs for the Council Chamber. Inscribed with instructions to the maker, Green & King, and still in use in their original setting.
Pencil dated Jany. 65
Collection: *Victoria and Albert Museum*
E.619–1963

2 Mayor's Chair: oak with carved and inlaid decoration upholstered in green leather. Made by Green & King, 1865.
Collection: *Northampton Town Hall*
H. 142 cm; W. 74 cm

3 Councillor's chair: oak with inlaid decoration upholstered in green leather. Made by Green & King, 1865.
Collection: *Northampton Town Hall*
H. 74 cm; W. 51 cm

4 'End of Dining Room shewing Buffet Dromore Castle near Limerick': original drawing for the illustration published in the *Architect*, 20 August 1870. The buffet is surmounted by a formalised peacock derived from a Japanese badge, the blue and white vase in the margin of the drawing presumably a real one used as a model. The upper part of the drawing shows the wall decoration intended to be painted by Henry Stacy Marks, RA, with medieval figures representing Chastity and Industry.
Pen and ink and wash, 1870
Collection: *British Architectural Library, RIBA, London*

5 'Art Furniture' working drawings for a whatnot and the Eagle Chair, including half-size peacock ornament and full-size eagle head, for Dromore Castle. Made in oak by William Watt, 1869.
Pen, ink and pencil
Collection: *British Architectural Library, RIBA, London*

6 Design and working drawing for a Chess Table for Dromore Castle. Made of ebonised mahogany, with boxwood pierced decorations and real ebony and boxwood squares on the playing surface. Made by William Watt, 1869.
Pen, ink, pencil and wash
Collection: *British Architectural Library, RIBA, London*

7 Designs for easy chairs, two sofas, whatnots, card tables, light chairs and a circular settee with a centre flower receptacle for Dromore Castle, 1869. The specification required that all should be made of mahogany ebonised by penetrating stain and dry polished. The upholstery to be done 'with yellow satin on colour like that known in China as Imperial Yellow' and the small chairs 'with plaited fine straw back'. The furniture made by William Watt, 1870.
Pen, ink and pencil
Collection: *British Architectural Library, RIBA, London*

8 Chair: ebonised wood with split cane seat and back panel. Designed in 1869 for Dromore Castle and made by William Watt, and in production with slight variations for about fifteen years. Illustrated in *Art Furniture*, William Watt, 1877 (Plates 2 and 8) and in advertisements for William Watt, Artistic Furniture Warehouse, in the *British Architect*, 1878.
Private Collection
H. 33 cm; W. 18 cm; D. 16 cm

9 Armchair of oiled wainscott oak with seat and back covered in natural leather with stamped pattern in gold. Designed in 1869 for Dromore Castle and made by William Watt, 1870.
Collection: *Victoria and Albert Museum*
Circ.719–1966
H. 108 cm; W. 62 cm; D. 74 cm

10 Bookcase: oiled wainscott oak with turned ornament and brass handles and fittings. One of a group of similar pieces, designed in 1869, for Dromore Castle and made by William Watt, 1870.
Collection: *Ivor Braka*
H. 223.5 cm; W. 121.9 cm; D. 54.6 cm

11 Frontispiece from the designer's own copy of *Art Furniture designed by Edward W. Godwin, FSA, and manufactured by William Watt, 21 Grafton Street, Gower Street, London*. Published in London in 1877 by B. T. Batsford, 52 High Holborn, on behalf of William Watt the catalogue was dedicated by permission to HRH Princess Louise for whom

Godwin designed and decorated a studio in the following year. A pencil sketch of a plan for the Anglo-Japanese entrance hall has been added in the margin.
Private Collection

12 Dining Room Furniture: Plate 6 from *Art Furniture* annotated by the designer with prices.
Private Collection

13 Anglo-Japanese Drawing Room Furniture: Plate 8 from *Art Furniture* annotated by the designer with prices.
Private Collection

14 Plate 14 from *Art Furniture* showing a complete interior scheme incorporating individual pieces of furniture annotated by the designer with prices. Godwin wrote in 'Description of Illustrations': 'The furniture and decoration throughout have been the result of a study of Japanese form adapted to modern English wants.'
Private Collection

15 'Old English or Jacobean' armchair: oak with a cane seat. Made by Collier & Plucknett of Warwick from a design made for William Watt about 1877. Illustrated in *Art Furniture* by William Watt (Plate 15 and on the cover). The designer wrote in 'Description of Illustrations': '"Jacobean furniture". The title is a misnomer, the furniture shown being no more Jacobean than that shown on Plate 8 is Japanese . . . what I have endeavoured to secure in design has been rather a modern treatment of certain well known and admired styles, than a mere reproduction of old forms.' As there is no recorded association between Godwin and Collier & Plucknett this seems to be an example of the plagiarism which led to the registration with the Patent Office of various designs made for Watt.
Collection: *Victoria and Albert Museum*
Circ.643–1962
H. 91.5 cm; W. 52 cm

16 Buffet: ebonised wood with silver-plated fittings and panels of embossed Japanese leather paper. Made by William Watt about 1876. Originally designed and made for Godwin's own use in 1867, the buffet was subsequently made over a period of years with minor variations in design and decoration, notably the buffet in the collection of the City of Bristol Museum and Art Gallery dated from 1867 which has six legs whereas this piece has eight. Illustrated in *Art Furniture* by William Watt (Plate 6), with the caption: 'This buffet as here shown was originally made for Mr Godwin in black and gold with a curtain of gold embroidery on yellow satin. It has also been made with a door in place of the curtain . . .'.
Collection: *Victoria and Albert Museum*
Circ.38–1953
H. 180 cm; W. 259 cm; D. 56 cm

17 Detail of cupboard door of buffet showing silver plated hinges and handles and Japanese leather paper. This was first imported into England by Liberty & Co, 1876.
Collection: *Victoria and Albert Museum*
Circ.38–1953

18 Coffee table: ebonised wood originally designed in 1867 and subsequently made by the Art Furniture Company, Collinson & Lock and William Watt working to Godwin's design. Illustrated *Art Furniture*, William Watt, 1877 (Plate 15 and on the cover).
Collection: *Victoria and Albert Museum*
W.71–1981
H. 66 cm; W. 40.50 cm

19 Coffee or occasional tables: ebonised wood designed by E. W. Godwin, or based on his design, about 1880. In the preface to *Art Furniture*, 1877, Godwin wrote of his designs having become so popular 'as to be copied by others in the trade but have unfortunately been travestied even caricatured in the process. A marked example of this is the

square coffee table you first made for me nine or ten years ago. The lines and dimensions of the different parts of what seems to be a very simple bit of furniture constitute its beauty and its art – if it has any. But I have seen the lines changed, the proportions altered, until that which I regarded as beauty became to me an offence and an eyesore.'
Collection: *Cecil Higgins Art Gallery, Bedford*
H. 66 cm; W. 43 cm; and H. 66 cm; W. 40 cm

20 Circular eight-legged table: ebonised wood with turned decoration and brass mounted legs or shoes. Designed about 1876 and made by William Watt. Illustrated *Art Furniture* (Plates 12 and 14) and described as available ebonised or in walnut with optional brass shoes extra.
Collection: *Victoria and Albert Museum*
W.54–1980
Diam. 99 cm; H. 76 cm

21 Octagonal eight-legged table: ebonised wood with turned and gilt decoration. Designed about 1876 and made by William Watt. An enamel label on reverse reads 'WILLIAM WATT, ART FURNITURE WAREHOUSE, 21 GRAFTON STREET, WC, GOW [ER] ST'.
Collection: *Cecil Higgins Art Gallery, Bedford*
Diam. 88.9 cm; H. 71.1 cm

22 Design for a circular eight-legged table with full size details. Inscribed 'for Watt' and dated by the artist Aug 14 '76.
Pencil and wash
Collection: *Victoria and Albert Museum*
E.494–1963

23 Designs from a sketchbook for two tables inscribed with notes and comments
Pen, ink and pencil, about 1875
Collection: *Victoria and Albert Museum*
E.278–1963
Page size 23 cm × 16.5 cm

24 Design for a sideboard from a sketchbook. The piece was made in pollard oak by Collinson &

Lock and exhibited at the Universal Exhibition, Vienna, 1873.
Pencil, dated Sunday Oct 11 '72
Collection: *Victoria and Albert Museum*
E.229–1963

25 Design for a cabinet book stand or Bibliothek from a sketchbook. The piece was made in ebony or ebonised wood relieved with gold and colour 'sparingly applied' by Collinson & Lock and exhibited at the Universal Exhibition, Vienna, 1873.
Pencil inscribed 'des Oct 1872 for Fletcher'
Collection: *Victoria and Albert Museum*
E.229–1963

26 Design for an armchair from a sketchbook inscribed 'chair for Esterhazy via Collinson & Lock Oct '73 Ordered in Vienna'. Notes in the sketchbook record orders 'Met Lock Golden Lamb Hotel Leopold Strasse Vienna Oct 18 1873'.
Pencil
Collection: *Victoria and Albert Museum*
E.234–1963

27 Designs for chairs in interior settings signed with the monogram EWG and inscribed 'Collinson & Lock Chairs for Vienna Oct '73'. Godwin's ledger for this period records the payment of £3 3s 0d each for designs for: Jap chair Vienna Oct 25 1873; Dining Room chair Princess Esterhazy Oct 10 1873.
Pen, ink and pencil on tracing paper
Provenance: Ellen Terry Memorial papers
Collection: *National Trust*

28 Contemporary photograph of part of the William Watt stand at the Universal Exhibition, Paris, 1878. The head board of the stand inscribed 'Designed by E. W. Godwin, Esq. Decorations Harmony in Yellow and Gold Designed and Painted by J. A. McN. Whistler, Esq. CHINA Lent by A. L. LIBERTY Regent Street.'
Collection: *Victoria and Albert Museum*

29 Original design from a sketchbook for the central feature of the Watt stand at the Universal Exhibition, Paris 1878. Inscribed 'Watt Paris 22 Sep '77'.
Pencil
Collection: *Victoria and Albert Museum*
E.233–1963

30 Sketches and notes by E. W. Godwin of the 'Peacock Room' originally at 49 Princes' Gate, London (now Freer Gallery, Washington). The room was designed by Thomas Jeckyll and decorated by Whistler, 1877. Godwin's sketches and comments are on a copy of the printed handout by Whistler describing his 'Harmony in Blue and Gold'. Inscribed '49 Princes' Gate at 6 o'clock 16 Feb '77'.
Pen, ink and pencil
Provenance: Miss Birnie Philip, sister of Mrs Beatrice Godwin, by whom bequeathed to *Hunterian Art Gallery, University of Glasgow*

31 Design for a chair with cane seat and back in the Japanese style, the chair made by William Watt and shown at the Universal Exhibition, Paris, 1878. Inscribed 'Wicker Chair $\frac{1}{4}$ real size' and signed and dated EWG Sep 77.
Pen and ink
Collection: *Victoria and Albert Museum*
E.479–1963

32 Design for a Music Bookcase, registered with the Patent Office by the maker 'William Watt Upholsterer 21 Grafton Street East Gower Street London' December 1877. Illustrated *Art Furniture* (Plate 8, called Music Wagon).
Pencil and wash
Collection: *Public Record Office, London*

33 Design for an Easy Chair or Settee, registered with the Patent Office by the maker, William Watt, November 1876. The chair made by William Watt was shown at the Universal Exhibition, Paris, 1878

as part of the Harmony in Yellow and Gold. Illustrated in the *Building News*, 14 June 1878 and *Art Furniture* (Plate 14).
Pencil and wash
Collection: *Public Record Office, London*

34 Easy Chair or Armchair: ebonised wood with upholstered back, arms and seat. The ivory disc showing Patent Office Registration of the design for 14 November 1876, attached on the underside of the chair. A variation on the registered design is the omission of the stretchers.
Private Collection

35 Contemporary photograph of a chair designed by H. H. Richardson in 1878 probably for the Public Library, Woburn, Massachusetts. This is one of a group of designs more or less directly related to the Godwin designs shown in Paris in 1878.
Collection: *Houghton Library, Harvard University*

36 Canterbury or Music Bookcase: walnut with brass drawer handle. A version of the design registered with the Patent Office in December 1876 by William Watt and made by him. An enamelled label on the reverse reading 'WILLIAM WATT GRAFTON STREET'.
Provenance: The home of E. W. Godwin and Ellen Terry and thence to their daughter, Edith Craig, by whom bequeathed to the *National Trust*
H. 62 cm; W. 56 cm; D. 30.5 cm

37 Design for a table, registered with the Patent Office by the maker William Watt, November 1876. The table made by William Watt was shown at the Universal Exhibition, Paris, 1878 as part of the Harmony in Yellow and Gold. Illustrated in *Art Furniture*, 1877 (Plate 8).
Pencil and wash
Collection: *Public Record Office, London*

38 Designs for tables from a sketchbook. Two variations on the design patented by William Watt in November 1876, inscribed 'Done Watt Dec 14 76'.
Pencil
Collection: *Victoria and Albert Museum*
E.233–1963

39 Table: mahogany, the top tiled with Minton tiles dated 1880. A heavier version of the elegant Watt table of 1876, the maker unknown.
Private Collection
H. 59 cm; W. 57 cm; D. 57 cm

40 Contemporary photograph of part of the Collinson & Lock stand at the Centennial Exhibition, Philadelphia, 1876. The Anglo-Japanese cabinet designed in 1874 is on the left of the picture and the sideboard or buffet and chair were also designed by Godwin.
Collection: *Free Library of Philadelphia*

41 Design for a Japanese Cabinet made of actual Japanese box panels framed in ebonised satinwood and mahogany with gilt metal mounts. The cabinet made by Collinson & Lock and exhibited at the Philadelphia Centennial Exhibition, 1876. Inscribed with instructions to the maker and signed E.W.G. July 2nd 74.
Pen and ink
Collection: *Victoria and Albert Museum*
E.478–1963

42 'Lucretia' corner cabinet: rosewood with incised and painted decoration designed about 1878. Made by Collinson & Lock, the decoration painted by Charles Fairfax Murray.
Collection: *Michael Whiteway*

43 Double Music Stool: ebonised birch, chestnut and pine with a cane seat. Designed for Godwin's own use about 1870, and probably made by William Watt.

Provenance: The home of E. W. Godwin and Ellen Terry and thence to their daughter, Edith Craig, by whom bequeathed to *Bristol Museum and Art Gallery*
H. 84.6 cm; W. 98.4 cm; D.40.9 cm

44 Hanging Bookcase: walnut, the lower brackets altered to allow the piece to stand on the floor. Designed for Godwin's own use about 1867 and made probably by William Watt.
Provenance: The home of E. W. Godwin and Ellen Terry and thence to their daughter, Edith Craig, by whom bequeathed to *Bristol Museum and Art Gallery*
H. 141.2 cm; W. 73.4 cm; D. 22.8 cm

45 Wardrobe: pine with turned wooden handles, about 1867. One of a reversed pair made for Godwin's own use, probably by the Art Furniture Company. Illustrated in *Art Furniture*, William Watt, 1877 (Plate 15). Writing in the *Architect*, 1 July 1876, Godwin said, 'The bedroom furniture was exceedingly plain. My wardrobe was a compound design – half chest of drawers and half hanging wardrobe and like the trouser patterns of some years ago, required a pair to show the complete design.'
Provenance: The home of E. W. Godwin and Ellen Terry and thence to their daughter, Edith Craig, by whom bequeathed to *Bristol Museum and Art Gallery*
H. 210.4 cm; W 120.4 cm; D. 47.2 cm

46 Designs for bedroom furniture from a sketchbook inscribed 'one of a pair of wardrobes'.
Pencil and wash, about 1873
Collection: *Victoria and Albert Museum*
E.233–1963

47 Wardrobe: ash with carved decoration, the decorative panels of the door and drawer fronts being rotary cut to reveal the figure of the wood. Designed and made about 1874. Stamped W. Watt,

26 Grafton Street, Gower Street, London W1.
Collection: *Victoria and Albert Museum*
W.75–1982
H. 213.5 cm; W. 162.5 cm; D. 65 cm

48 Designs for bedroom or toilet sets from a sketch-book inscribed '⅛ real size'. Designed probably in 1876 for W. Brownfield, Cobridge, Staffs, the makers for William Watt. The two-handled set illustrated in *Art Furniture*, William Watt, 1877 (Plate 16).
Pencil and watercolour
Collection: *Victoria and Albert Museum*
E.233–1963

49 Design for a dressing table from a sketchbook inscribed 'gave to S. & E. for self Oct 6 79'. The makers S. & E. have so far been unidentified.
Collection: *Victoria and Albert Museum*
E.233–1963

50 Dressing Table: oak with brass handles and escutcheon, designed 1879, and made by William Watt as part of a group of bedroom furniture illustrated in the *Building News*, 24 October 1879, with descriptive text 'They are made of oak and are simple, practical pieces of furniture whose lines have been determined chiefly by the use for which they are intended.'
Provenance: Ellen Terry and then to her daughter, Edith Craig, by whom bequeathed to the *National Trust*
H. 72.5 cm; W.106.5 cm; D. 79 cm

51 Design for a revolving bookcase from a sketch-book inscribed 'Watt pd'. Designed about 1879 and made by William Watt. Illustrated in the *Building News*, 31 October 1879, with descriptive text 'The "companion book-stand" is a novel contrivance having four sides, and turning on a centre which stands on a tripod, so that a considerable number of books may be consulted by a reader who may be sitting at a writing table, without quitting his seat.'
Pencil
Collection: *Victoria and Albert Museum*
E.233–1963

52 Design for a couch in classical style with full size details. Signed E.W.G. and dated Apl 9 73. Inscribed 'inlay of ivory and ebony if wood is of light colour or ivory and brass if dark or ebonised'.
Pencil and wash
Collection: *Victoria and Albert Museum*
E.493–1963

53 Sideboard, chairs and revolving stool from a sketchbook about 1876. The designs made probably by William Watt, the stool illustrated in *Art Furniture*, William Watt, 1877 (Plate 12).
Pencil and wash
Collection: *Victoria and Albert Museum*
E.233–1963

54 Drawings of furniture details based on museum studies from a sketchbook, about 1876.
Pencil and wash
Collection: *Victoria and Albert Museum*
E.233–1963

55 Design for a sideboard from a sketchbook dated 30 July 76. A version of this design illustrated in *Art Furniture*, William Watt, 1877 (Plate 15, called 'Old English or Jacobean').
Pencil and watercolour
Collection: *Victoria and Albert Museum*
E.233–1963

56 Design for a Cottage Angle Cabinet from a sketchbook. Dated Apl 23rd 1874 and inscribed with a list of other work for Collinson & Lock including three pieces for Grey Towers.
Pencil
Collection: *Victoria and Albert Museum*
E.235–1963

57 Designs for Japanese-style coffee tables with detailed drawings of 'delicate inlaid work', 1874. Inscribed 'Grey Towers' and instructions for the makers, Collinson & Lock.
Pencil and wash
Collection: *Victoria and Albert Museum*
E.487–1963

58 Designs for Anglo-Japanese hanging cabinets from a sketchbook, about 1877.
Pencil and wash
Collection: *Victoria and Albert Museum*
E.229–1963

59 Designs for a cabinet, table, leg of a couch and a drawer handle from a sketchbook, about 1881.
Pencil and watercolour
Collection: *Victoria and Albert Museum*
E.423–1963

60 Designs from a sketchbook for a chair, an occasional table and alternative legs inscribed 'Anglo Egyptian' and 'sold to Waugh Nov 1876'.
Pen, ink and pencil
Collection: *Victoria and Albert Museum*
E.233–1963

61 Table: lacquered wood with painted, incised and gilt decoration of Egyptian inspiration designed probably by E. W. Godwin about 1876.
Collection: *Ivor Braka*
H. 71 cm; L. 91.5 cm; D. 53.5 cm

62 Studies of antique chairs and stools inscribed with details of materials and decoration and BM (British Museum), about 1875.
Pen and ink
Collection: *Victoria and Albert Museum*
E.278–1963

63 Designs for chairs from a sketchbook, about 1873.
Pencil and wash
Collection: *Victoria and Albert Museum*
E.229–1963

64 'Greek' chair: ebonised oak with upholstered seat and back, about 1885. Illustrated in the *Building News*, 18 December 1885, as part of a group of inexpensive furniture 'executed by representatives of the late Mr William Watt'. Three versions of the chair were available of which this was the more expensive. Version B 'all plain and no moulding' and Version C 'cut square legs as well as uprights'.
Collection: *Victoria and Albert Museum*
Circ.258–1958
H. 107 cm; W. 61 cm

65 Notes of furniture details from the 'Parthenon Marbles' and a 'Dictionnaire des Arts Grècques', about 1883. The precision of these drawings suggests that the Parthenon Marbles sketches were taken from published illustrations rather than from the actual Elgin Marbles.
Pencil
Collection: *Victoria and Albert Museum*
E.472–1963

66 Designs from a sketchbook for a table and a chair back in the Musharabîyeh manner, about 1883.
Pencil
Collection: *Victoria and Albert Museum*
E.432–1963

67 Sheet of designs for a sofa by Dante Gabriel Rossetti. The notes on the design are in the hand of William Morris and the sofa was made for Morris, Marshall, Faulkner & Co and exhibited at the International Exhibition, London, 1862. Described by Charles Dickens in *All the Year Round* as 'a sofa . . . straight and angular and stuffed possibly with discarded horse-hair shirts' and in

the *Builder*, 14 June 1862, as 'a sofa of hard white polished wood with black rings'. The sofa was the only known forerunner of Godwin's simple shapes of five years later both based presumably on a mutual knowledge of Japanese woodcuts.
Pen, ink and pencil
Collection: *Birmingham Museums and Art Gallery*

68 Armchair: oak from the Shakespere [sic] Dining-Room Set comprising three chairs, a table and a sideboard, the latter registered with the Patent Office, 14 November 1881, and made by William Watt. An enamel label inscribed 'William Watt Grafton Street' on the underside. Illustrated in the *Building News*, 11 November 1881, and in production for several years. 'The Shakespeare chair is now in every upholsterer's showroom' according to a writer in *The Cabinet Maker*, vol VII, 1885/6, p.260.
Provenance: Ellen Terry and thence to her daughter, Edith Craig, by whom bequeathed to the *National Trust*
H. 102 cm; W. 61.5 cm; D. 47 cm

69 Drawing for the illustration 'Outline of Interior Decoration' by E. W. Godwin published in the *British Architect*, July 1881.
Brown ink on tracing paper
Private Collection
H. 28.5 cm; W. 46 cm

70 Design for a small house drawn on the reverse of the frontispiece of E. W. Godwin's own copy of *Art Furniture*, William Watt, 1877. Inscribed with costs and notes, the design incorporates a version of the entrance hall and stairs of the frontispiece illustration.
Private Collection
H. 19 cm; W. 21 cm

71 Section through a house with a female figure, fireplace and sketch design inscribed 'brick wall above rail'. Possibly Godwin's own house, Fallows Green, Harpenden, about 1871.
Pen, ink, pencil and watercolour
Collection: *British Architectural Library, RIBA, London*

72 Sketch of a drawing room, signed E.W.G. and dated Sep.73. Inscribed 'The whole room is suggested by the Garden in the "Romance of the Rose" therefore artists engaged in panels etc to be refered to Chaucers poem.' The room was to be panelled in rosewood, the upper walls with gold and black pattern on a dark vellum ground and the inscription round the room at dado height to be 'lines 2289 to 2292 Chaucers Romaunt of the Rose'.
Pen and ink on tracing paper
Private Collection
H. 10 cm; W. 21 cm

73 Sketch designs from a letter to HRH Princess Louise, for windows, an alcove and a fireplace in her proposed studio at Kensington Palace. Signed E. W. Godwin and dated Aug 31 78.
Pen and ink
Private Collection
H. 18 cm; W. 22 cm

74 'October': one of a series of designs for figures emblematic of the months used as the *British Architect Kalender* for 1881. Some of the designs are from an earlier date since 'October' was used as the design for the Autumn figure on the painted panels of the cabinet (colour plate 10) made by William Watt in 1877.
Pencil and watercolour
Collection: *Victoria and Albert Museum*
E.530–1963

75 Drawings of Japanese powderings or crests from a sketchbook mainly devoted to Japanese-based designs, about 1870. All these crests provided the motifs for pattern design, notably the peacock,

the peach blossom, the sparrows and the butterfly.
Pencil and wash
Collection: *Victoria and Albert Museum*
E.280–1963

76 'Butterfly Brocade': silk damask designed in about 1874 and woven by Warner & Son exclusively for Collinson & Lock.
Collection: *Victoria and Albert Museum*
T.152–1972

77 Design for part of the Peacock wallpaper made for Jeffrey & Co and registered with the Patent Office, 1872. Signed E.W.G. and inscribed 'to be printed in the pale ground tint on the darkest or line tint, the second that for the making of the feathers'. Produced by Jeffrey & Co, 1873. Illustrated in *Art Furniture*, William Watt, 1877, alternatively as a filling and a frieze.
Pencil and watercolour on tracing paper
Collection: *Victoria and Albert Museum*
E.513–1963
Diam. 29.5 cm

78 One of a series of 'Wall-Paper Decorations' advertising the firm of Jeffrey & Co, illustrated in the *Building News*, 8 May 1874, showing the Sparrow frieze, Bamboo filling (colour plate 15) and Peacock dado.
Collection: *Victoria and Albert Museum*

79 Design for Sparrow frieze and a floral filling made for Jeffrey & Co, 1872. Illustrated in *Art Furniture*, William Watt, 1877 (Plate 20).
Pencil on tracing paper
Collection: *Victoria and Albert Museum*
E.514–1963
35.6 cm × 35.8 cm

80 Design for tiles signed E.W.G. and inscribed 'Japanese', about 1870.
Pencil and blue wash
Collection: *Victoria and Albert Museum*
E.380–1963

81 Design for a Greek wallpaper from a sketchbook containing mainly ideas for textiles and wallpapers, about 1877.
Pencil and watercolour
Collection: *Victoria and Albert Museum*
E.241–1963

82 Designs for wallpapers from a sketchbook containing mainly ideas for textiles and wallpapers, about 1877. The designs inscribed 'Daisy' and 'Moth Pattern'.
Pencil and watercolour
Collection: *Victoria and Albert Museum*
E.241–1963

83 'Apple' wallpaper designed for William Watt and registered by him with the Patent Office in 1876. The design was sold to Watt on 11 May 1876, together with two other papers called 'Queen Anne' and 'Star'. The producer of the papers is not known, though the quality of the printing suggests Jeffrey & Co.
Collection: *Public Record Office, London*

84 'Star' wallpaper designed for William Watt and registered by him with the Patent Office in 1876.
Collection: *Public Record Office, London*

85 'Nagasaki': silk damask designed in about 1874 and woven by Warner & Sons.
Collection: *Victoria and Albert Museum*
Circ.297–1953

Plates

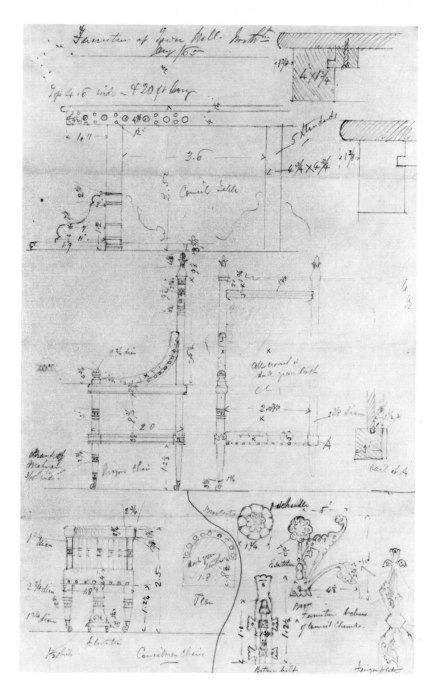

1 Designs for furniture
for Northampton Town
Hall, 1865
*Victoria and Albert
Museum*

2 Mayor's chair, 1865
Northampton Town Hall

36

3 Councillor's chair,
1865
Northampton Town Hall

4 Design for a buffet
and wall decoration,
Dromore Castle, 1870
*British Architectural
Library, RIBA, London*

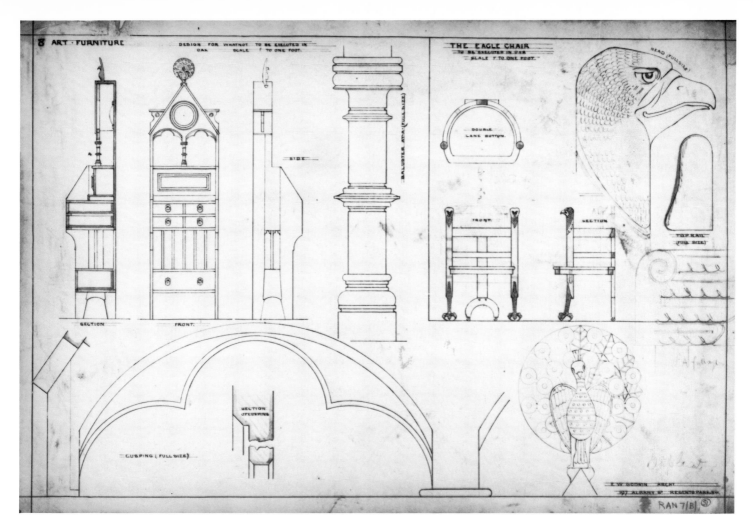

5 Drawings for 'Art
Furniture' for Dromore
Castle, 1869
*British Architectural
Library, RIBA, London*

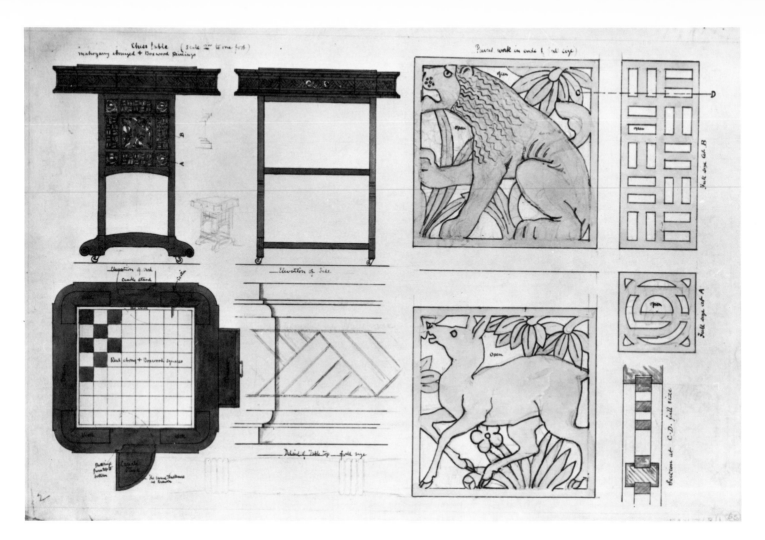

6 Drawings for furniture
for Dromore Castle, 1869
*British Architectural
Library, RIBA, London*

40

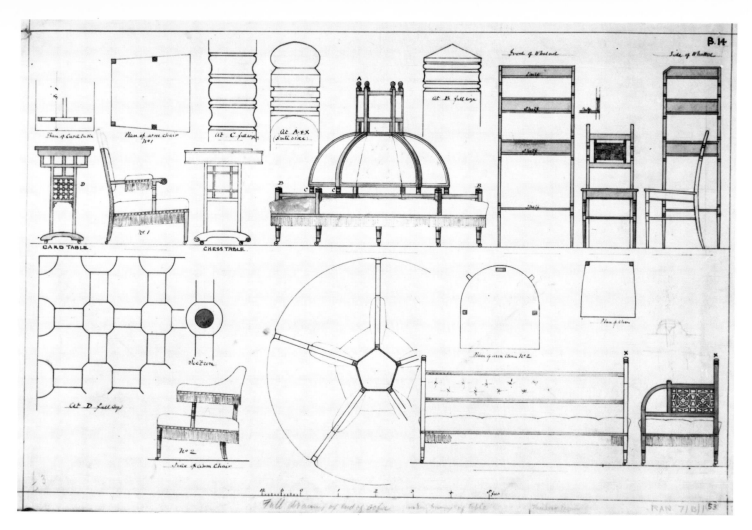

7 Drawings for furniture
for Dromore Castle, 1869
*British Architectural
Library, RIBA, London*

41

8 Chair designed about
1869
Private Collection

9 Armchair designed for
Dromore Castle, 1869
*Victoria and Albert
Museum*

10 Bookcase designed
for Dromore Castle, 1869
Ivor Braka

11 Frontispiece of 'Art
Furniture from Designs
by E. W. Godwin FSA
and others', a catalogue
published in 1877
Private Collection

T.WAY, PHOTO-LITH, 21, WELLINGTON ST, STRAND, W.C.

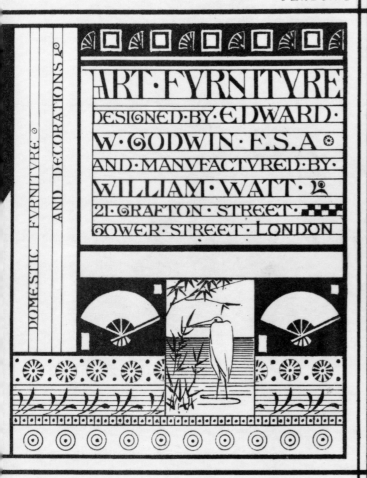

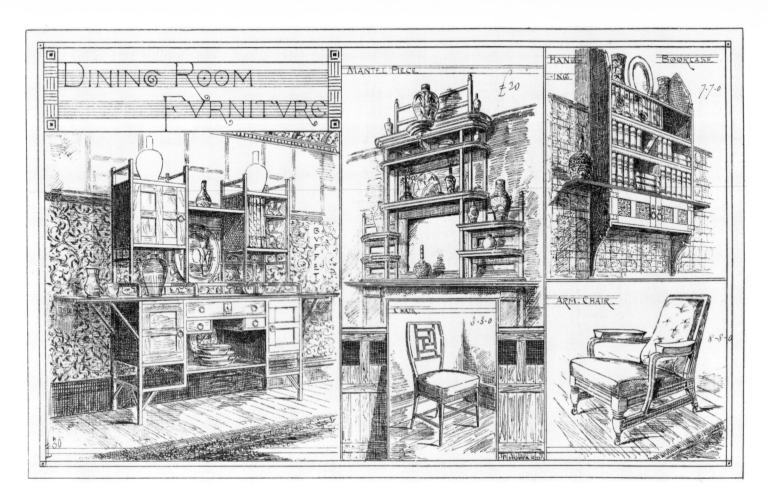

12 Dining Room
Furniture, Plate 6 from
the catalogue, 1877
Private Collection

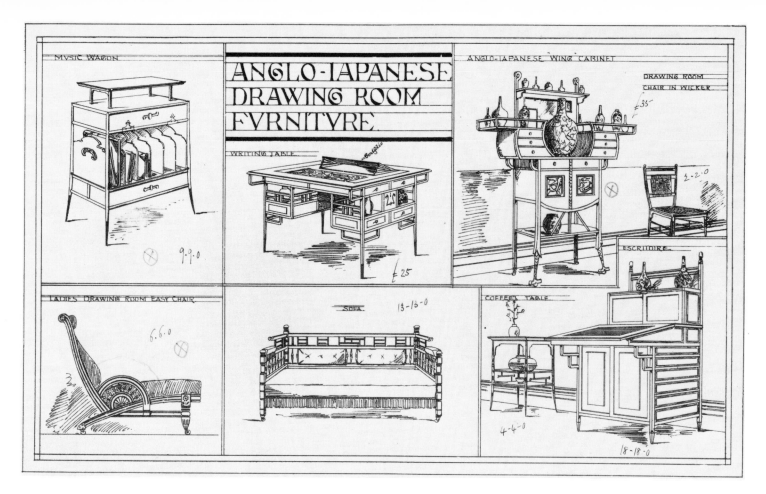

13 Anglo–Japanese
Drawing Room
Furniture, Plate 8 from
the catalogue, 1877
Private Collection

14 An interior scheme,
Plate 14 from the
catalogue, 1877
Private Collection

8·8·0   2·2·0   15·15·0
15·15·0   6·6·

5·5·0

f 34

ART FVRNITVRE WAREHOVSE,
21, GRAFTON STREET, GOWER STREET, LONDON.

15 'Old English or
Jacobean' armchair,
designed about 1877
*Victoria and Albert
Museum*

17 Detail of the
cupboard door of the
buffet, about 1876
*Victoria and Albert
Museum*

18 Coffee Table, ebonised
wood, about 1876
*Victoria and Albert
Museum*

16 Buffet, ebonised
wood, about 1876
*Victoria and Albert
Museum*

19 Coffee or occasional
tables, about 1880,
based, by unidentified
makers, on the original
Godwin design of 1867
*Cecil Higgins Art Gallery,
Bedford*

20 Circular eight-legged
table, about 1876
*Victoria and Albert
Museum*

21 Octagonal eight-
legged table, about 1876
*Cecil Higgins Art Gallery,
Bedford*

22 Design from a
sketchbook, 1876
*Victoria and Albert
Museum*

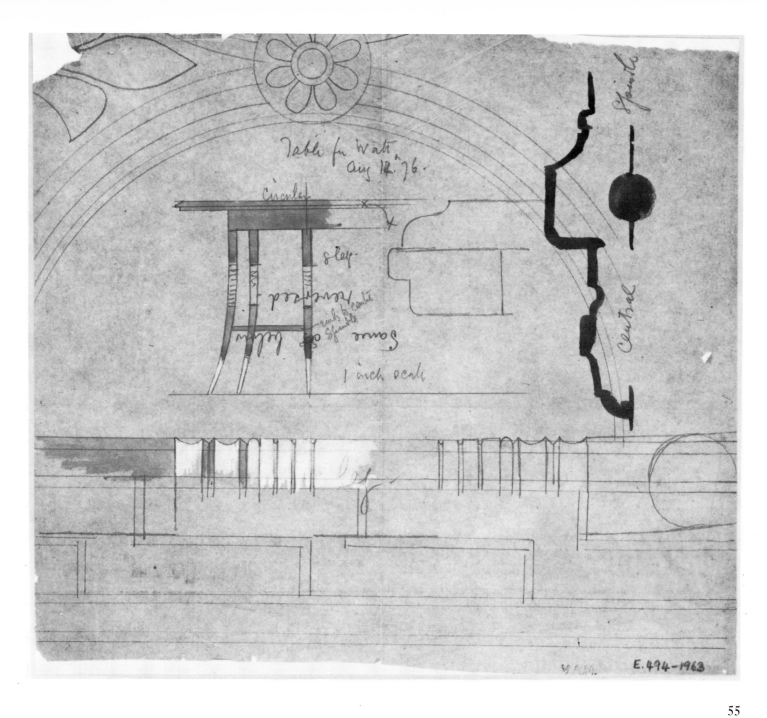

Table for Watts
Aug 18 76.

Circular

S leg

restored

inch ½ centre
Spindle

Some of litter

1 inch scale

Spindle

Central

55

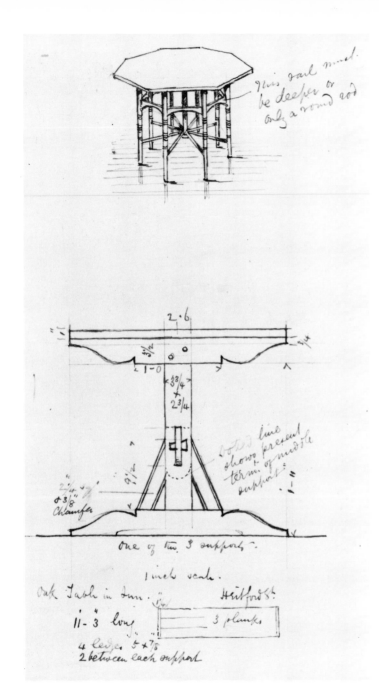

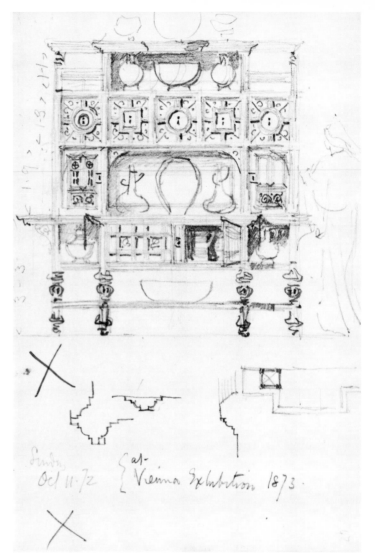

23 Designs from a
sketchbook, about 1875
*Victoria and Albert
Museum*

24 Design from a
sketchbook, 1872
*Victoria and Albert
Museum*

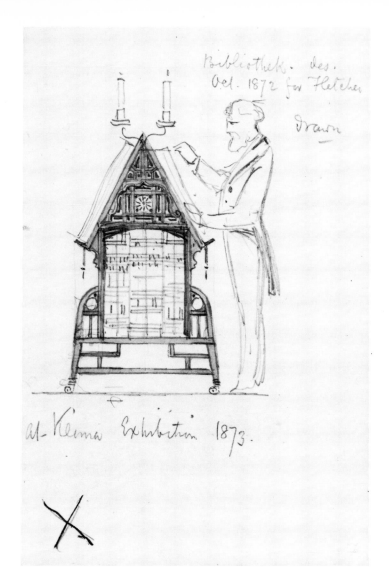

Bibliothek. des.
Oct. 1872 for Fletcher

Drawn

at Vienna Exhibition 1873.

25 Design from a
sketchbook, 1872
*Victoria and Albert
Museum*

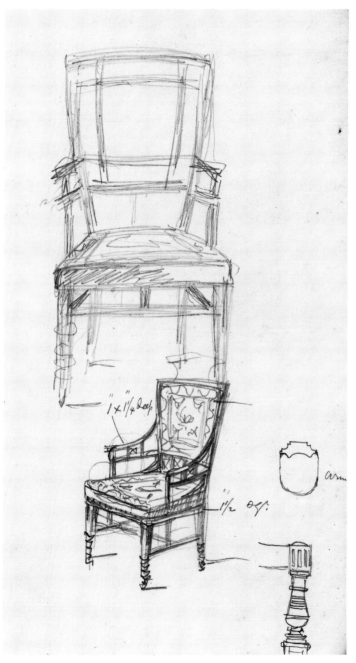

26 Design from a
sketchbook, 1873
*Victoria and Albert
Museum*

57

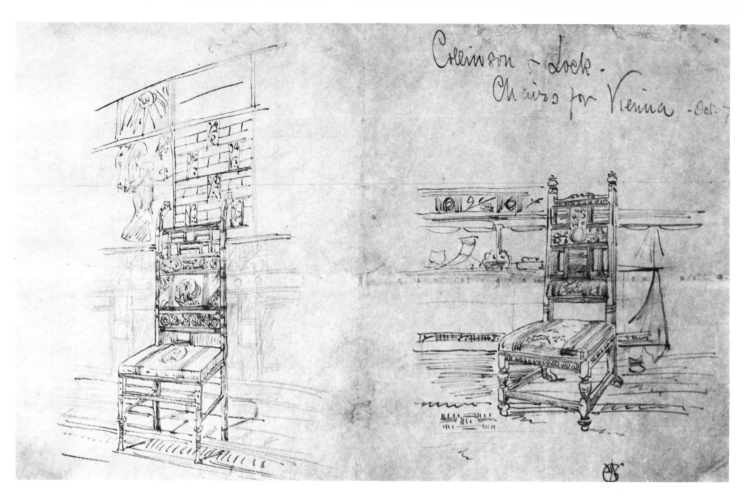

27 Designs for chairs
and their settings, 1873
National Trust

28 The William Watt
stand, Universal
Exhibition, Paris, 1878
*Victoria and Albert
Museum*

29 Design from a
sketchbook for the
'Butterfly Cabinet', 1877
*Victoria and Albert
Museum*

59

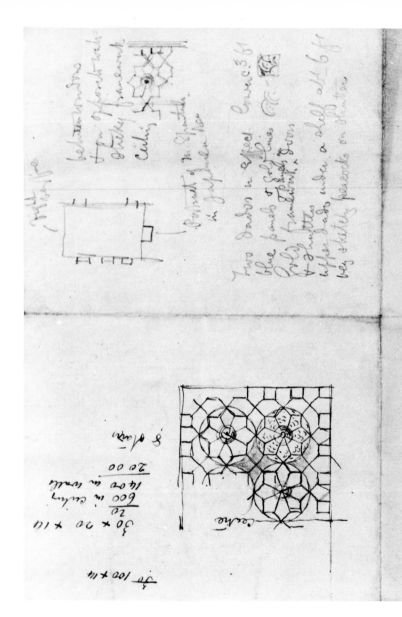

"HARMONY IN BLUE AND GOLD.
THE PEACOCK ROOM."

The Peacock is taken as a means of carrying out this arrangement.

A pattern, invented from the Eye of the Peacock, is seen in the ceiling spreading from the lamps. Between them is a pattern devised from the breast-feathers.

These two patterns are repeated throughout the room.

In the cove, the Eye will be seen running along beneath the small breast-work or throat-feathers.

On the lowest shelf the Eye is again seen, and on the shelf above—these patterns are combined: the Eye, the Breast-feathers, and the Throat.

Beginning again from the blue floor, on the dado is the breast-work, BLUE ON GOLD, *while above, on the Blue wall, the pattern is reversed,* GOLD ON BLUE.

Above the breast-work on the dado the Eye is again found, also reversed, that is GOLD ON BLUE, *as hitherto* BLUE ON GOLD.

The arrangement is completed by the Blue Peacocks on the Gold shutters, and finally the Gold Peacocks on the Blue wall.

30 Sketches and notes
by E. W. Godwin on a
visit to the 'Peacock
Room', 1877
*Hunterian Art Gallery,
University of Glasgow*

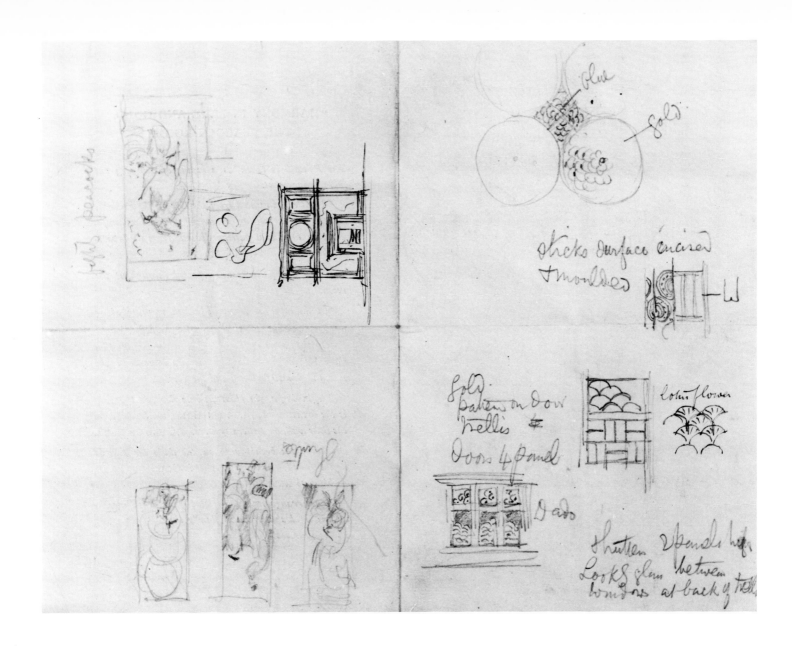

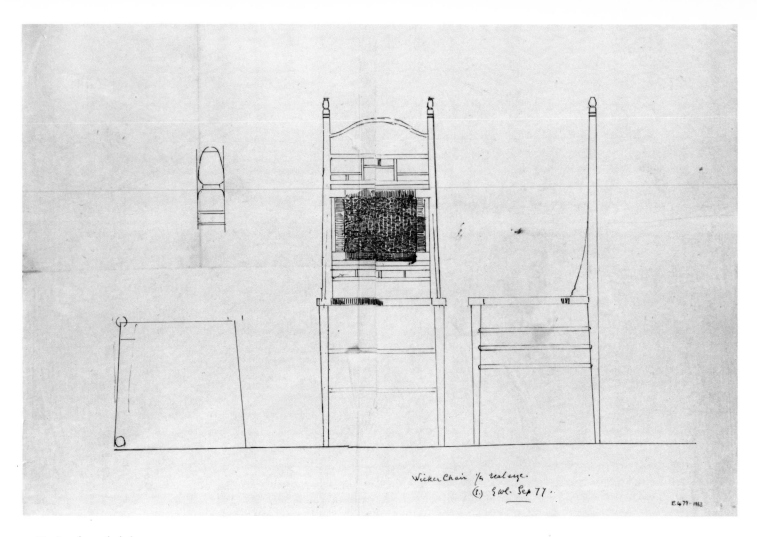

Wicker Chair ¼ real size.
(E.) E.W.G. Sep 77.

E.479-1962

31 Design for a chair in
the Japanese style, 1877
*Victoria and Albert
Museum*

32 Design for a Music
Bookcase, 1877
Public Record Office

34 (over) Easy Chair or
Armchair, 1876
Private Collection

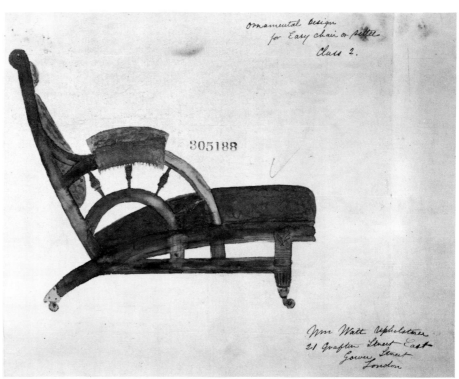

33 Design for an Easy
Chair or Settee, 1876
Public Record Office

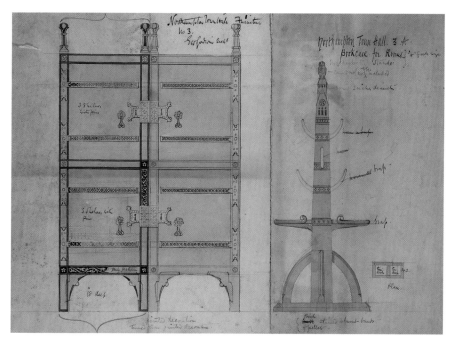

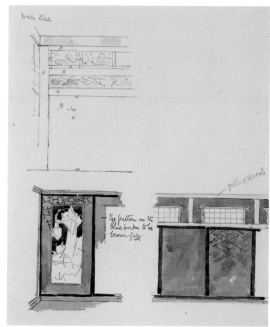

1 Designs for a bookcase
and umbrella stand at
Northampton Town
Hall, about 1863
*Victoria and Albert
Museum*

3 Design for interior
decoration in the
Japanese manner,
about 1875
*Victoria and Albert
Museum*

2 Designs for a Japanese
wall decoration for
Dromore Castle, County
Limerick, about 1869
*Victoria and Albert
Museum*

4 Design from a
sketchbook for a small
display cabinet, about
1876
*Victoria and Albert
Museum*

5 Design from a
sketchbook for a fireplace
and surround called
'Persian Romance',
about 1878
*Victoria and Albert
Museum*

6 Design from a
sketchbook for the
'Monkey Cabinet' and a
coffee table, about 1876
*Victoria and Albert
Museum*

7 Design from a
sketchbook for an Anglo-
Japanese cabinet in a
room setting, about 1877
*Victoria and Albert
Museum*

8 'Monkey Cabinet':
walnut with carved
boxwood insets and ivory
handles in the form of
monkeys, about 1876
*Victoria and Albert
Museum*

9 'Butterfly Cabinet':
designed by E. W.
Godwin and decorated
by J. A. McNeill
Whistler, 1878
*Hunterian Art Gallery,
University of Glasgow*

10 Cabinet: satinwood
with brass mounts and a
carcass of mahogany, the
upper doors decorated
with four painted and
gilt panels representing
the seasons, 1877
*Victoria and Albert
Museum*

11 Design from a
sketchbook for the
'Beatrice Cabinet' and
stand, about 1879
*Victoria and Albert
Museum*

12 Design from a
sketchbook for decorative
panels for a cabinet,
about 1878
*Victoria and Albert
Museum*

13 Design for a panel of
stained or painted glass,
about 1877
*Victoria and Albert
Museum*

14 Design for a roundel
of stained glass, about
1867
*Victoria and Albert
Museum*

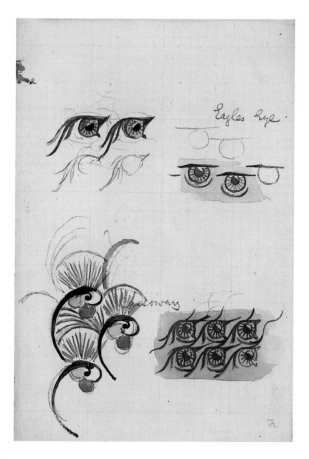

15 Designs from a
sketchbook based on
birds' eyes, about 1877
*Victoria and Albert
Museum*

16 Design for the
Bamboo wallpaper,
dated 1872
*Victoria and Albert
Museum*

17 Figure in an Anglo-
Japanese room setting
from a notebook, about
1876
*Victoria and Albert
Museum*

18 'Lucretia' corner
cabinet, 1873
Michael Whiteway

35 Contemporary
photograph of a chair
designed by H. H.
Richardson, 1878
*Houghton Library,
Harvard University*

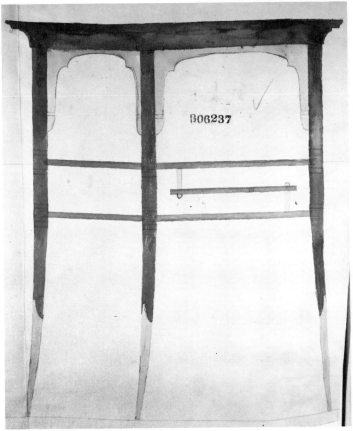

36 Canterbury or Music
Bookcase, walnut, 1876
National Trust

37 Design for a table,
1876
Public Record Office

66

38 Designs from a
sketchbook, 1876
*Victoria and Albert
Museum*

39 Table, mahogany
with a tiled top, about
1880
Private Collection

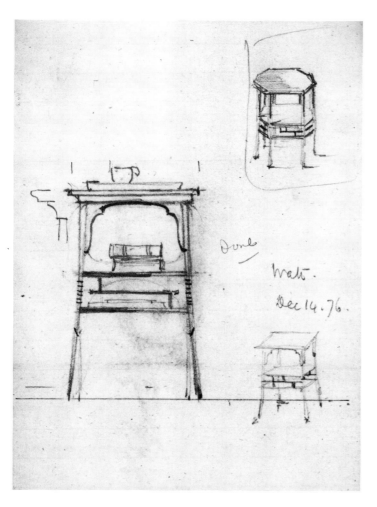

40 Part of the Collinson
& Lock stand,
Centennial Exhibition,
Philadelphia, 1876
*Free Library of
Philadelphia, USA*

41 Design for a Japanese
Cabinet, 1874
*Victoria and Albert
Museum*

42 Door and centre
panel of 'Lucretia'
corner cabinet, 1873
Michael Whiteway

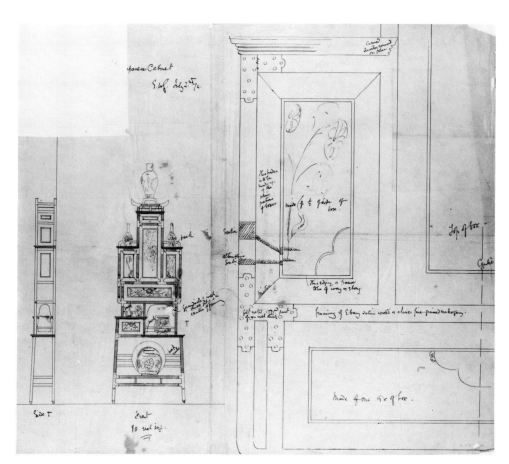

69

43 Double Music Stool,
ebonised birch, about
1870
Bristol Museum and
Art Gallery

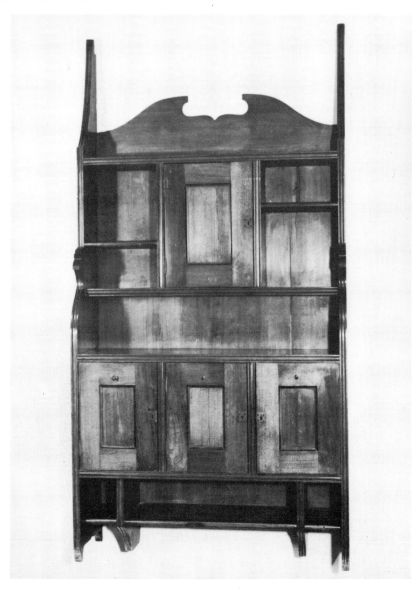

44 Hanging Bookcase,
walnut, about 1867
*Bristol Museum and
Art Gallery*

45 Wardrobe, pine,
about 1867
*Bristol Museum and
Art Gallery*

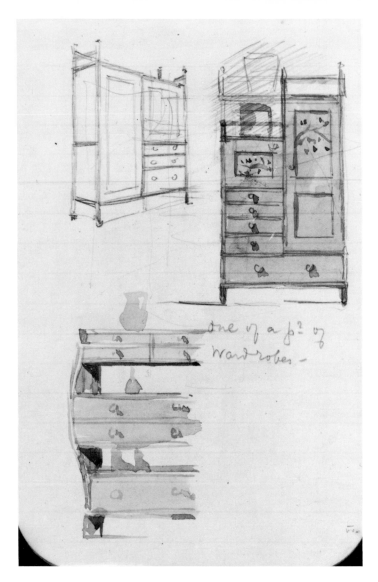

46 Designs from a
sketchbook, about 1873
*Victoria and Albert
Museum*

47 Wardrobe, ash,
about 1874
*Victoria and Albert
Museum*

48 Designs from a
sketchbook, about 1876
*Victoria and Albert
Museum*

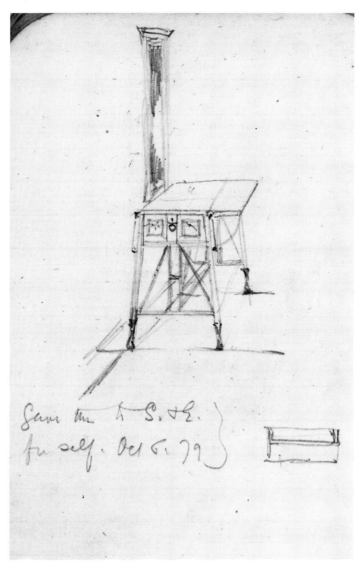

49 Design from a
sketchbook, 1879
*Victoria and Albert
Museum*

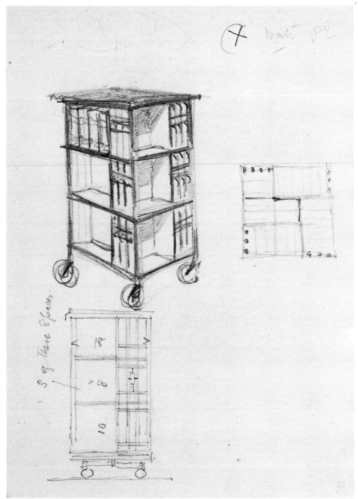

50 Dressing Table, oak,
1879
National Trust

51 Design from a
sketchbook, about 1879
*Victoria and Albert
Museum*

74

52 Design for a couch,
1873
*Victoria and Albert
Museum*

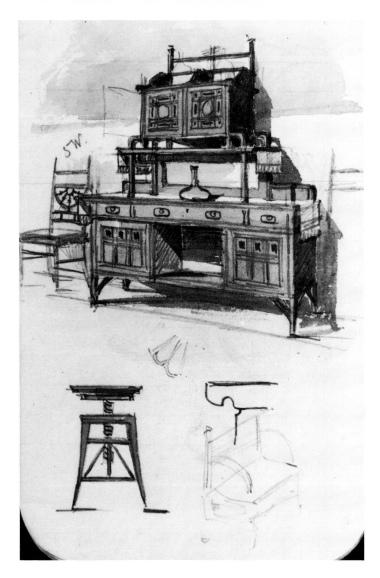

53 Designs from a
sketchbook, about 1876
*Victoria and Albert
Museum*

54 Museum studies
from a sketchbook,
about 1876
*Victoria and Albert
Museum*

55 Design from a
sketchbook, 1876
*Victoria and Albert
Museum*

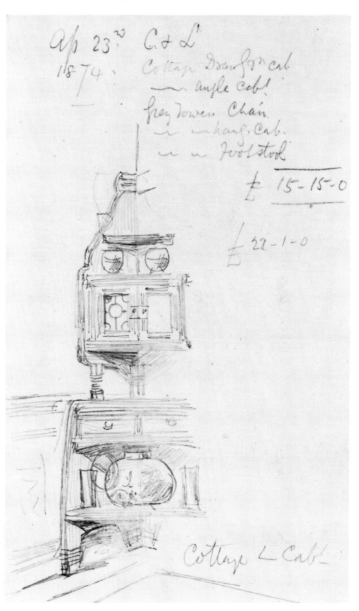

56 Design from a
sketchbook, 1874
*Victoria and Albert
Museum*

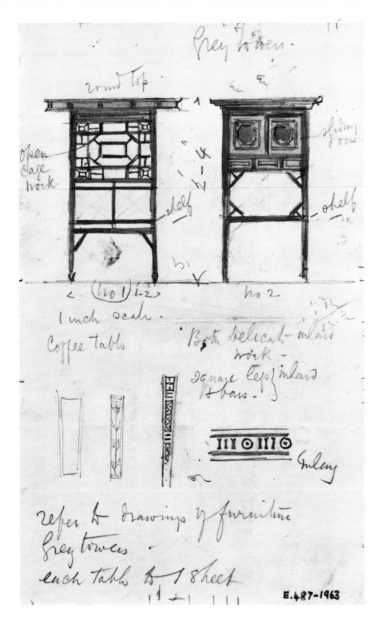

57 Designs for coffee
tables, 1874
*Victoria and Albert
Museum*

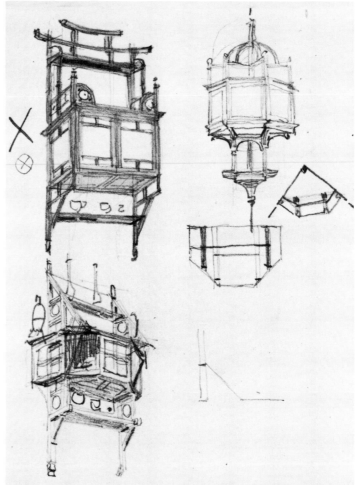

58 Designs from a
sketchbook, about 1877
*Victoria and Albert
Museum*

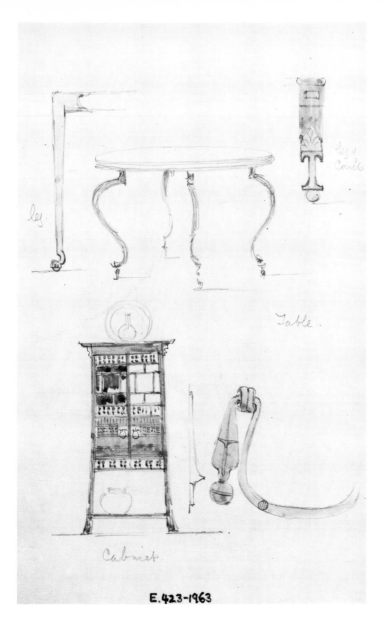

E.423-1963

59 Designs from a
sketchbook, about 1881
*Victoria and Albert
Museum*

60 Designs from a
sketchbook, 1876
*Victoria and Albert
Museum*

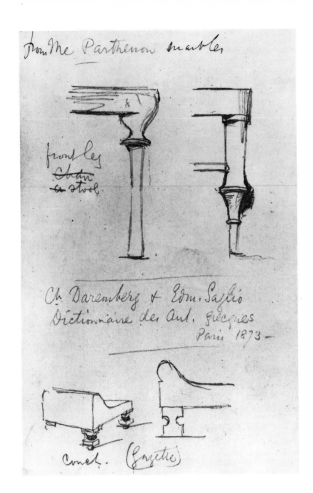

65 Notes of furniture
from the 'Parthenon
Marbles', about 1883
*Victoria and Albert
Museum*

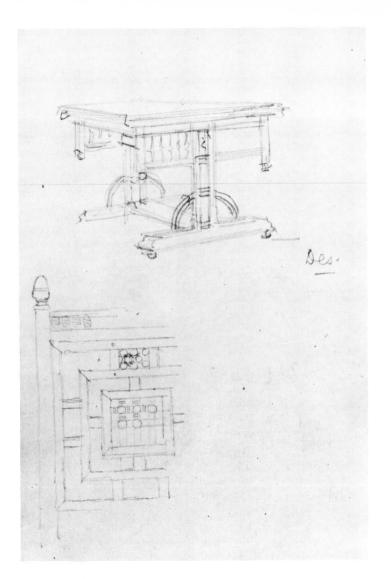

66 Designs from a
sketchbook, about 1883
*Victoria and Albert
Museum*

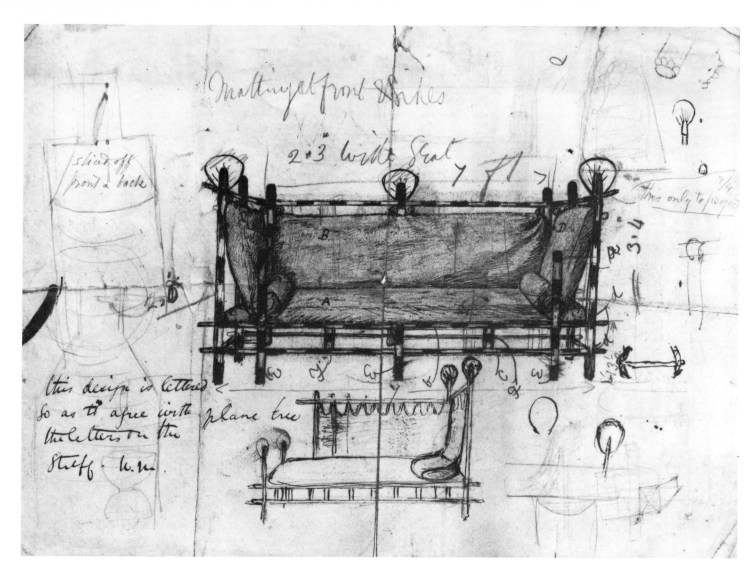

67 Designs for a sofa by
Dante Gabriel Rossetti,
about 1862
*Birmingham Museums
and Art Gallery*

68 The Shakespere
Armchair, oak, 1881
National Trust

70 Design for a small
house, about 1877
Private Collection

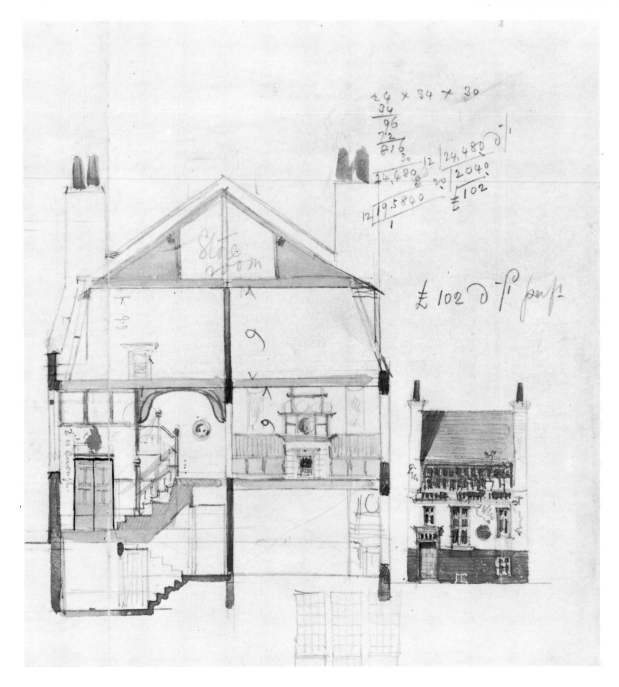

86

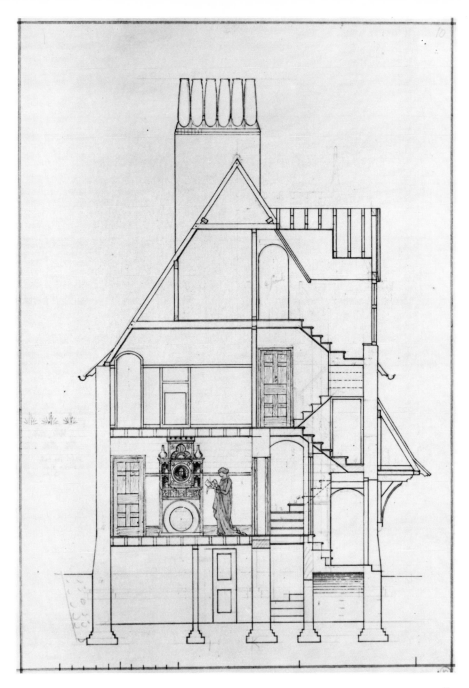

71 Section through a
house showing interior
decoration, about 1871
*British Architectural
Library, RIBA, London*

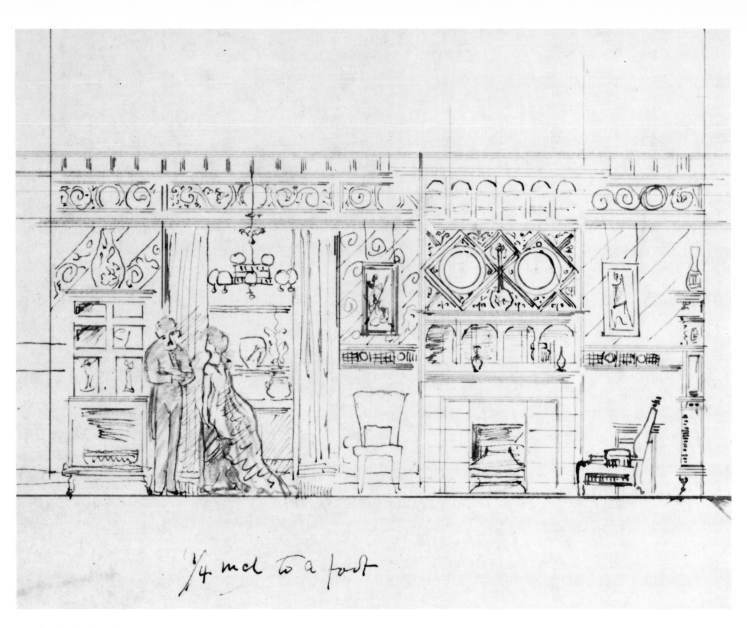

72 Sketch of a drawing
room, 1873
Private Collection

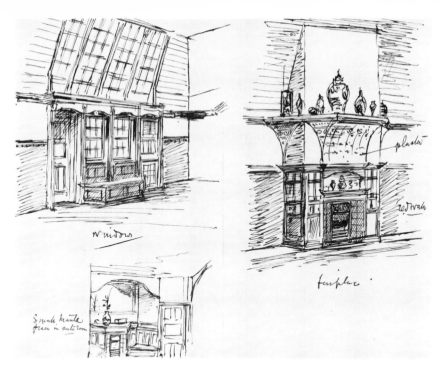

73 Sketches for a studio
for HRH Princess
Louise, 1878
Private Collection

74 'October': one of a
series of months, about
1877
*Victoria and Albert
Museum*

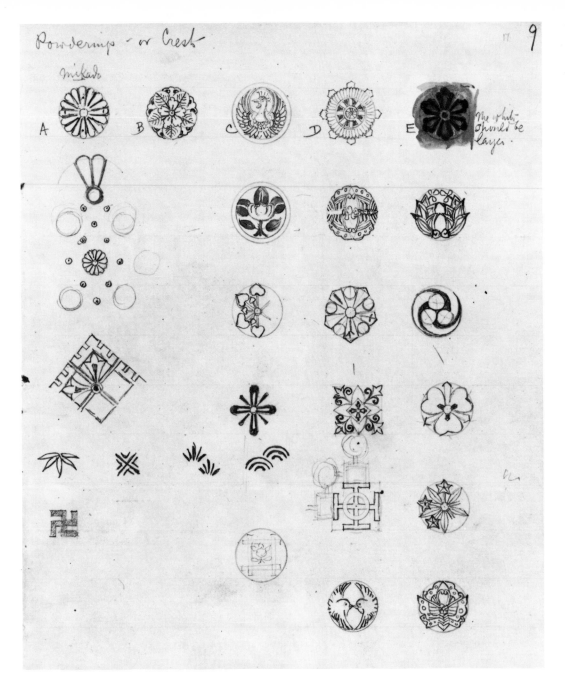

75 Drawings of Japanese
crests, about 1870
*Victoria and Albert
Museum*

77 Design for the
Peacock wallpaper, 1872
*Victoria and Albert
Museum*

76 'Butterfly Brocade',
silk damask, about 1874
*Victoria and Albert
Museum*

91

78 'Wall-Paper
Decorations' made by
Jeffrey & Co, 1874
*Victoria and Albert
Museum*

79 Design for Sparrow
frieze and floral filling,
1872
*Victoria and Albert
Museum*

80 Design for tiles,
about 1870
*Victoria and Albert
Museum*

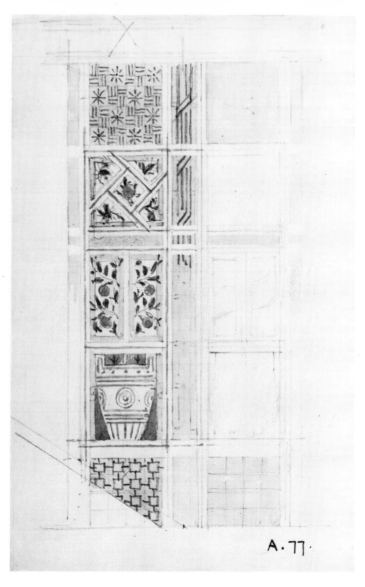

A.77.

81 Design for a
wallpaper from a
sketchbook, about 1877
*Victoria and Albert
Museum*

93

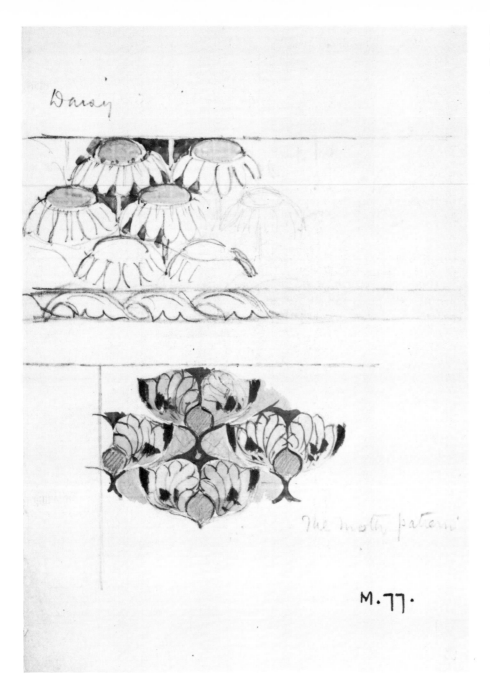

Daisy

The moth pattern

M.77.

82 Designs for wallpaper
motifs from a sketchbook,
about 1877
*Victoria and Albert
Museum*

94

83 'Apple' wallpaper,
1876
Public Record Office

84 'Star' wallpaper, 1876
Public Record Office

85 'Nagasaki', silk
damask, about 1874
Victoria and Albert
Museum